Air Fryer Cookbook

AIR FRYER
MAGIC

*The One-Stop Keto Air Fryer
Recipes Cookbook With Low Oil
Yet Crispy and Delicious Meat
and Vegetable Meals For Everyone*

RACHEL HOUSTON

Table of Contents

PART I

Air Fryer Recipes

The air fryer is a new mode of cooking advertised as a guilt-free and healthy way of enjoying all your favorite foods. Air fryer cooking claims that it can lower the fat content of various well-known food items such as chicken wings, French fries, fish sticks, and others. But, how healthy is it to cook in an air fryer?

Air fryer is a trendy appliance in the kitchen today that is being used for making food items like pastries, meat, and potato chips. It functions by simply circulating the hot air all around the food for producing crispy and crunchy exterior. All those food items that are air-fried are believed to be great alternatives for the deep-fried food items. There is no need to submerge the food items in oil. Just brush some oil, and you are good to go. It has been found that air fryer can cut off the fat content by 75%. The main reason behind this is that they need less amount of fat in comparison to deep fryers. For example, most of the deep-fried food items will require three cups of oil. But, the same can be cooked in an air fryer with only one tbsp. of oil.

In case you are willing to trim some extra fat around your waistline, substituting deep-fried food items with air-fried food items is a great way to start. So, it can be said that air-fryer can help in promoting weight loss. Frying food can produce dangerous compounds such as acrylamide. Cooking food in an air fryer can help you cut down the acrylamide content in your cooking. I have included some tasty air fryer recipes in this chapter that can be made with minimal effort.

Chapter 1: Chicken And Pork Recipes

Meat forms an essential part of most types of diet. Here are some chicken and pork recipes that can be made easily using an air fryer.

Maple Chicken Thighs

Total Prep & Cooking Time: One hour and thirty-five minutes

Yields: Four servings

Nutrition Facts: Calories: 410 | Protein: 22.3g | Carbs: 47.9g | Fat: 12.3g | Fiber: 1.2g

Ingredients

- One cup of buttermilk
- One large egg
- Half cup of maple syrup
- One tsp. of garlic (granulated)
- Four chicken thighs

For the dry mix:

- Half cup of flour
- One-fourth cup of tapioca flour
- One tbsp. of salt

- One tsp. of each
  - Sweet paprika
  - Onion (granulated)
  - Honey powder
- Half tsp. of paprika (smoked)
- One-fourth tsp. of each
  - Garlic (granulated)
  - Cayenne powder
  - Black pepper (ground)

Method:

1. Mix maple syrup, buttermilk, egg, and one tsp. of granulated garlic in a bowl. Add the thighs of chicken and marinate them for one hour.

2. Mix tapioca flour, flour, sweet paprika, salt, smoked paprika, pepper, granulated onion, half tsp. of granulated garlic, cayenne, and honey powder in a bowl.

3. Preheat your air fryer at 190 degrees Celsius.

4. Drain the marinade. Add the thighs in the flour mixture. Placechicken thighs in the air fryer basket. Cook them for ten minutes. Flip the chicken thighs and cook again for ten minutes.

Buttermilk Chicken
Total Prep & Cooking Time: Thirty-five minutes

Yields: Four servings

Nutrition Facts: Calories: 331 | Protein: 23.2g | Carbs: 26.3g | Fat: 10.6g | Fiber: 0.8g

Ingredients

- One cup of buttermilk
- Half tsp. of each
  - Hot sauce
  - Garlic salt
  - Paprika
  - Oregano
  - Onion powder
- One-third cup of tapioca flour
- One-eighth tsp. of black pepper (ground)
- One large egg
- Half cup of flour
- Two tsps. of brown sugar
- One tsp. of garlic powder
- One-fourth tsp. of black pepper
- One pound of chicken thighs (skinless, boneless)

Method:

1. Take a shallow dish and mix hot sauce with buttermilk.

2. Combine garlic salt, tapioca flour, and one-eighth tsp. of black pepper. Mix well.

3. Beat the egg in a bowl.

4. Mix salt, flour, brown sugar, paprika, garlic powder, onion powder, one-fourth tsp. of black pepper, and oregano in a bowl. Combine well.

5. Dip the thighs of chicken in this order: mixture of buttermilk, mixture of tapioca flour, beaten egg, and flour mixture.

6. Preheat your air fryer at 190 degrees Celsius. Use parchment paper for lining the fryer basket.

7. Cook the chicken thighs for ten minutes. Flip the thighs and cook again for ten minutes.

Cheddar-Stuffed BBQ Breasts of Chicken

Total Prep & Cooking Time: Thirty-five minutes

Yields: Two servings

Nutrition Facts: Calories: 370 | Protein: 35.7g | Carbs: 11.7g | Fat: 17.7g | Fiber: 0.6g

Ingredients

- Three bacon strips
- Two ounces of cheddar cheese (cubed)
- One-fourth cup of barbeque sauce
- Two chicken breasts (skinless)
- Pepper and salt

Method:

1. Preheat your air fryer to 190 degrees Celsius. Cook a bacon strip in the air fryer for two minutes. Chop one strip of bacon. Use parchment paper for lining the fryer basket.

2. Mix cooked bacon, one tbsp. of barbeque sauce, and cheddar cheese.

3. Create a one-inch pouch at the top of the chicken breasts. Stuff the pouch with the mixture of bacon and cheese.

4. Wrap the bacon strips around the breasts of chicken. Use barbeque sauce for coating the chicken breasts.

5. Cook for ten minutes in the air fryer. Flip the chicken breasts and cook again for ten minutes.

Buffalo Chicken

Total Prep & Cooking Time: Forty minutes

Yields: Four servings

Nutrition Facts: Calories: 230 | Protein: 30.2g | Carbs: 21.1g | Fat: 4.7g | Fiber: 1.9g

Ingredients

- Half cup of Greek yogurt
- One-fourth cup of egg substitute
- One tbsp. of each
  - Hot sauce
  - Sweet paprika
  - Cayenne pepper
  - Garlic pepper seasoning
- One tsp. of hot sauce
- One cup of bread crumbs
- One pound of chicken breast

Method:

1. Mix egg substitute, yogurt, and hot sauce in a mixing bowl.

2. Combine paprika, bread crumbs, cayenne pepper, and garlic pepper in a dish.

3. Dip the chicken breasts into the mixture of yogurt and coat in the mixture of bread crumbs.

4. Cook the chicken breasts in the air fryer for eight minutes. Flip the chicken breasts and cook again for five minutes.

Breaded Pork Chops

Total Prep & Cooking Time: Twenty minutes

Yields: Four servings

Nutrition Facts: Calories: 390 | Protein: 41.7g | Carbs: 10.3g | Fat: 17.1g | Fiber: 0.9g

Ingredients

- Four pork chops
- One tsp. of Cajun seasoning
- Two cups of garlic and cheese flavored croutons
- Two large eggs
- One cooking spray

Method:

1. Place the chops in a dish and season with the Cajun seasoning.

2. Add the croutons in a blender and pulse them.

3. Beat the eggs in a shallow dish.

4. Dip the pork chops into the beaten eggs and then coat in the blended croutons.

5. Use a cooking spray for misting the pork chops.

6. Cook the chops for five minutes. Flip the chops and cook again for five minutes.

Pork Meatballs

Total Prep & Cooking Time: Thirty-five minutes

Yields: Twelve servings

Nutrition Facts: Calories: 120 | Protein: 8.4g | Carbs: 3.9g | Fat: 7.7g | Fiber: 0.3g

Ingredients

- Twelve ounces of pork (ground)
- Eight ounces of Italian sausage (ground)
- Half cup of panko bread crumbs
- One large egg
- One tsp. of each
  - Parsley (dried)
  - Salt
- Half tsp. of paprika

Method:

1. Combine sausage, pork, egg, bread crumbs, salt, paprika, and parsley in a bowl. Mix well. Make twelve meatballs using your hands.

2. Place the meatballs in the basket of the air fryer basket. Cook them for eight minutes. Shake the fryer basket and cook again for two minutes.

Pork Jerky

Total Prep & Cooking Time: Eleven hours and ten minutes

Yields: Forty servings

Nutrition Facts: Calories: 56 | Protein: 4.4g | Carbs: 0.2g | Fat: 4.6g | Fiber: 0.1g

Ingredients

- Two pounds of pork (ground)
- One tbsp. of each
  - o Sesame oil
  - o Sriracha
  - o Soy sauce
  - o Rice vinegar
- Half tsp. of each
  - o Salt
  - o Black pepper
  - o Onion powder
  - o Pink curing salt

Method:

1. Mix pork, sriracha, sesame oil, soy sauce, vinegar, pepper, salt, onion powder, and curing salt in a bowl. Mix well and refrigerate for eight hours.

2. Use a jerky gun for making as many jerky sticks as possible.

3. Cook the jerky sticks in the fryer rack for one hour.

4. Flip the sticks and cook again for one hour.

5. Repeat step number four for three hours.

6. Transfer the sticks to a paper towel and soak excess fat.

7. Serve immediately, or you can store the sticks in the refrigerator for one month.

Pork Skewers

Total Prep & Cooking Time: Forty minutes

Yields: Forty servings

Nutrition Facts: Calories: 310 | Protein: 21g | Carbs: 30.6g | Fat: 9.2g | Fiber: 8.9g

Ingredients

- Two tbsps. of white sugar

- Five tsps. of onion powder
- Four tsps. of thyme (dried, crushed)
- One tbsp. of each
    o Black pepper (ground)
    o Allspice (ground)
    o Vegetable oil
    o Honey
    o Cilantro (chopped)
- Two tsps. of each
    o Salt
    o Cayenne pepper
- Three-fourth tsp. of nutmeg (ground)
- One-fourth tsp. of cloves (ground)
- One-fourth cup of coconut (shredded)
- One pound of pork tenderloin (cut in cubes of one inch)
- Four skewers
- One mango (peeled, chopped)
- Half a can of black beans (rinsed)
- One cup of red onion (chopped)
- Three tbsps. of lime juice
- One-eighth tsp. of black pepper (ground)

Method:

1. Mix onion powder, sugar, allspice, thyme, black pepper, salt, cayenne pepper, cloves, and nutmeg in a bowl. Transfer the prepared rub to another bowl and reserve one tbsp. for the pork. Add shredded coconut to the one tbsp. of rub and mix.

2. Preheat your air fryer to 175 degrees Celsius.

3. Start threading the chunks of pork onto the skewers. Use some oil for brushing the pork and then sprinkle the rub on all sides. Place the prepared skewers in the air fryer basket.

4. Cook for eight minutes.

5. Mash one-third of the mango in a bowl and add black beans, lime juice, onion, remaining mango, cilantro, honey, pepper, and salt.

6. Serve the pork skewers with mango mixture by the side.

Pork Tenderloin With Mustard Crust

Total Prep & Cooking Time: Forty minutes

Yields: Forty servings

Nutrition Facts: Calories: 280 | Protein: 24.3g | Carbs: 30.2g | Fat: 6.1g | Fiber: 4.9g

Ingredients

- One-fourth cup of Dijon mustard
- Two tbsps. of brown sugar
- One tsp. of parsley flakes
- Half tsp. of thyme (dried)
- One-fourth tsp. of each
  - Black pepper (ground)
  - Salt
- Two pounds of pork tenderloin
- One pound of small potatoes
- Twelve ounces of green beans (trimmed)
- One tbsp. of olive oil

Method:

1. Start by preheating your air fryer at 200 degrees Celsius.

2. Combine brown sugar, mustard, thyme, parsley, pepper, and salt together in a bowl. Coat the tenderloins with the marinade evenly on all sides.

3. Combine green beans, potatoes, and olive oil in another bowl. Use pepper and salt for seasoning.

4. Cook the pork for twenty minutes. Flip the pork and cook again for five minutes.

5. Let the pork sit for ten minutes.

6. Cook potatoes and green beans for ten minutes in the air fryer.

7. Serve pork with green beans and potatoes by the side.

Chapter 2: Beef And Fish Recipes

There are various types of beef and fish recipes that can be made using an air fryer. Let's have a look at them.

Beef Tenderloin

Total Prep & Cooking Time: One hour

Yields: Eight servings

Nutrition Facts: Calories: 230.2 | Protein: 31.2g | Carbs: 0.2g | Fat: 10.3g | Fiber: 0.1g

Ingredients

- Two pounds of beef tenderloin
- One tbsp. of each
  - Oregano (dried)
  - Vegetable oil
- One tsp. of salt
- Half tsp. of black pepper (cracked)

Method:

1. Preheat your air fryer at 200 degrees Celsius.

2. Use a paper towel to dry the beef tenderloin.

3. Drizzle some oil over the tenderloin and sprinkle pepper, oregano, and salt. Rub all the spices along with the oil evenly on the meat.

4. Reduce the air fryer heat to 190 degrees Celsius and cook the beef for twenty minutes. Reduce the air fryer heat to 180 degrees Celsius. Cook again for ten minutes.

5. Let the beef rest for ten minutes.

6. Slice the tenderloin and serve warm.

Beef Wontons

Total Prep & Cooking Time: Thirty minutes

Yields: Twenty-four servings

Nutrition Facts: Calories: 73.2 | Protein: 4.4g | Carbs: 5.9g | Fat: 2.6g | Fiber: 0.3g

Ingredients

- One pound of lean beef (ground)
- Two tbsps. of green onion (chopped)
- Half tsp. of each
  - Garlic powder
  - Salt
- One-fourth tsp. of each
  - Ginger (ground)
  - Black pepper (ground)
- Sixteen ounces of wonton wrappers
- Two tbsps. of sesame oil

Method:

1. Mix green onions, beef, garlic powder, salt, ginger, and pepper in a large bowl.

2. Preheat your air fryer at 175 degrees Celsius.

3. Place the wrappers on a large plate.

4. Take one tbsp. of the prepared beef mixture and add it to the wonton wrapper. Wet your finger with some water and fold the wrappers in half for forming a triangle.

5. Use sesame oil for brushing each side of the prepared wontons.

6. Cook them in the air fryer for four minutes.

7. Serve hot.

Mushrooms and Steak
Total Prep & Cooking Time: Four hours and fifty minutes

Yields: Forty servings

Nutrition Facts: Calories: 220 | Protein: 19.1g | Carbs: 5.7g | Fat: 12g | Fiber: 0.7g

Ingredients

- One pound of beef sirloin steak (cut in cubes of one inch)
- Eight ounces of button mushrooms (sliced)
- One-fourth cup of Worcestershire sauce
- One tbsp. of olive oil
- One tsp. of parsley flakes
- Half tsp. of paprika
- One-third tsp. of chili flakes (crushed)

Method:

1. Mix mushrooms, steak, olive oil, Worcestershire sauce, paprika, parsley, and chili flakes in a mixing bowl. Refrigerate the mixture for four hours.

2. Take out the mixture thirty minutes prior to your cooking.

3. Preheat your air fryer at a temperature of 200 degrees Celsius.

4. Drain all the marinade. Place the mushrooms and steak into the air fryer basket.

5. Cook for five minutes. Toss the mixture and cook again for five minutes.

Rib Eye Steak

Total Prep & Cooking Time: Two hours and twenty-five minutes

Yields: Two servings

Nutrition Facts: Calories: 650 | Protein: 41.3g | Carbs: 7.2g | Fat: 48.1g | Fiber: 0.9g

Ingredients

- Two rib-eye steaks
- Four tsps. of grill seasoning
- One-fourth cup of olive oil
- Half cup soy sauce

Method:

1. Mix soy sauce, steak, seasoning, and olive oil in a large bowl. Marinate the steaks for two hours.

2. Add one tbsp. of water to the base of the basket for preventing smoking at the time of cooking.

3. Preheat to 200 degrees Celsius.

4. Add the marinated steaks and cook for seven minutes. Flip the steaks and cook again for seven minutes.

5. Let the steaks it for five minutes.

6. Serve warm.

Meatloaf

Total Prep & Cooking Time: Forty-five minutes

Yields: Forty servings

Nutrition Facts: Calories: 290 | Protein: 23.8g | Carbs: 5.6g | Fat: 17.6g | Fiber: 0.9g

Ingredients

- One pound of lean beef (ground)
- One large egg (beaten)
- Three tbsps. of bread crumbs
- One onion (chopped)
- One tbsp. of thyme (chopped)
- One tsp. of salt
- Half tsp. of black pepper (ground)
- Two mushrooms (sliced thick)
- Half tbsp. of olive oil

Method:

1. Start by preheating the air fryer at 200 degrees Celsius.

2. Mix egg, beef, bread crumbs, thyme, onion, pepper, and salt together in a bowl. Mix well.

3. Transfer the mixture of beef to the basket and use a spatula for smoothening the top. Take the mushrooms and press them at the top. Coat the loaf with some olive oil.

4. Set the timer to twenty-five minutes.

5. Let the meatloaf sit for ten minutes.

6. Slice in wedges and serve.

Fish Sticks

Total Prep & Cooking Time: Twenty minutes

Yields: Forty servings

Nutrition Facts: Calories: 183.2 | Protein: 25.6g | Carbs: 15.2g | Fat: 4.4g | Fiber: 0.9g

Ingredients

- One pound of cod fillets
- One-fourth cup of flour
- One large egg
- Half cup of bread crumbs
- One cup of parmesan cheese (grated)
- One tbsp. of parsley flakes
- One tsp. of paprika
- Half tsp. of black pepper (ground)
- One serving of cooking spray

Method:

1. Start by preheating your air fryer at 200 degrees Celsius.

2. Use paper towels for pat drying the fillets of fish. Cut the fillets into sticks of half an inch.

3. Add flour in a flat dish.

4. Break the egg and beat in a separate bowl.

5. Combine cheese, bread crumbs, paprika, parsley, and pepper in another dish.

6. Coat the fish sticks in flour and then dip in egg. Coat the sticks with bread crumb mixture.

7. Use a cooking spray for greasing the basket of the air fryer. Arrange the fish stick in the basket.

8. Cook for five minutes. Turn the sticks and cook again for five minutes.

9. Serve hot.

Cajun Salmon
Total Prep & Cooking Time: Twenty minutes

Yields: Two servings

Nutrition Facts: Calories: 321 | Protein: 31.7g | Carbs: 4.2g | Fat: 17.2g | Fiber: 0.6g

Ingredients

- Two fillets of salmon
- One serving of cooking spray
- One tbsp. of Cajun seasoning
- One tsp. of brown sugar

Method:

1. Dry the fish fillets using paper towels.

2. Use a cooking spray for misting the fillets.

3. Mix Cajun seasoning along with brown sugar in a bowl. Transfer the mixture into a flat dish.

4. Press the fillets of fish into the mixture of spices.

5. Spray the air fryer basket with cooking spray. Place the fillets with the skin-side down.

6. Cook the fish for eight minutes.

7. Let the fish sit for two minutes.

8. Serve hot.

Salmon Cakes and Sriracha Mayo
Total Prep & Cooking Time: Forty minutes

Yields: Four servings

Nutrition Facts: Calories: 329 | Protein: 24.3g | Carbs: 3.5g | Fat: 23.2g | Fiber: 2.5g

Ingredients

For sriracha mayo:

- One tbsp. of sriracha
- One-fourth cup of mayonnaise

For salmon cakes:

- One pound fillets of salmon (cut in pieces of one inch)
- One-third cup of almond flour
- One large egg (beaten)
- Two tsps. of seafood seasoning
- One green onion (chopped)
- One serving of cooking spray

Method:

1. Mix sriracha and mayonnaise in a bowl. Reserve one tbsp. of the mayo and refrigerate the rest.

2. Add almond flour, salmon, one and a half tsps. of seafood seasoning, egg, reserve sriracha mayo, and green onion to a food processor. Pulse the ingredients for five minutes.

3. Line a dish with parchment paper. Make eight patties from the mixture of fish. Chill the patties in the refrigerator for ten minutes.

4. Preheat your air fryer at 200 degrees Celsius. Use a cooking spray for greasing the basket.

5. Mist the patties with cooking spray and place them in the basket.

6. Cook for eight minutes.

7. Serve the salmon cakes with sriracha mayo by the side.

Cod With Sesame Crust and Snap Peas

Total Prep & Cooking Time: Thirty minutes

Yields: Four servings

Nutrition Facts: Calories: 356 | Protein: 30.2g | Carbs: 21.3g | Fat: 14.1g | Fiber: 7.2g

Ingredients

- Four fillets of cod
- One pinch of black pepper and salt
- Three tbsps. of butter (melted)
- Two tbsps. of sesame seeds
- One tbsp. of vegetable oil
- Two packs of snap peas
- Three garlic cloves (sliced thinly)
- One orange (cut in wedges)

Method:

1. Use vegetable oil for brushing the basket of the air fryer. Preheat at 200 degrees Celsius.

2. Sprinkle the fillets of cod with some pepper and salt.

3. Mix sesame seeds and butter in a bowl.

4. Toss garlic and peas with some butter.

5. Cook the peas in the air fryer for ten minutes.

6. Brush the fillets of fish with the mixture of butter and cook for four minutes. Flip the fillets and brush with the remaining butter mixture. Cook again for five minutes.

7. Serve the fish fillets with orange wedges and snap peas.

Grilled Fish and Pesto Sauce

Total Prep & Cooking Time: Twenty minutes

Yields: Two servings

Nutrition Facts: Calories: 1012 | Protein: 44.3g | Carbs: 3.2g | Fat: 93g | Fiber: 2.1g

Ingredients

- Two fillets of white fish
- One tsp. of olive oil
- Half tsp. of each
    o Black pepper (ground)
    o Salt

For the pesto sauce:

- One bunch of basil
- Two cloves of garlic
- One tbsp. of pine nuts
- Two tbsps. of parmesan cheese (grated)
- One cup of olive oil (extra virgin)

Method:

1. Heat your air fryer at 180 degrees Celsius.

2. Brush the fillets of fish with some oil. Sprinkle salt and pepper.

3. Cook the fish fillets for eight minutes.

4. Add garlic, basil leaves, cheese, pine nuts, and olive oil in a blender. Pulse the ingredients until a thick sauce forms.

5. Serve the fish fillets with pesto sauce from the top.

6.

Chapter 3: Vegetarian Party Recipes

Besides cooking meat in an air fryer, you can also cook various vegetarian dishes with its help. In this section, you will find some tasty vegetarian dishes that you can make with the help of an air fryer.

Apple Pies
Total Prep & Cooking Time: Forty-five minutes

Yields: Four servings

Nutrition Facts: Calories: 476 | Protein: 3.3g | Carbs: 58.7g | Fat: 27.6g | Fiber: 3.6g

Ingredients

- Four tbsps. of butter
- Six tbsps. of brown sugar
- One tsp. of cinnamon (ground)
- Two apples (diced)
- Half tsp. of cornstarch
- Two tsps. of cold water
- Half package of pastry
- One serving of cooking spray
- Half tbsp. of grapeseed oil
- One-fourth cup of powdered sugar
- One tsp. of milk

Method:

1. Mix butter, apples, brown sugar, and ground cinnamon in a bowl. Add the mixture to a skillet and cook for five minutes until the apples are soft.

2. Combine cornstarch in water. Add the cornstarch mixture to the skillet.

3. Cook for one minute and keep aside.

4. Unroll the pastry crust and roll it out on a work surface with some flour. Cut the flattened dough in rectangles.

5. Place some apple filling at the center of each rectangle and fold the rectangles for sealing the pie.

6. Use a sharp knife for cutting small slits at the top.

7. Brush some oil at the top and cook for eight minutes at 195 degrees Celsius.

8. Combine milk and sugar in a bowl.

9. Serve the warm pies with sugar glaze from the top

Fruit Crumble

Total Prep & Cooking Time: Thirty minutes

Yields: Two servings

Nutrition Facts: Calories: 308 | Protein: 2.3g | Carbs: 47.9g | Fat: 7.2g | Fiber: 5.3g

Ingredients

- One medium-sized apple
- Half cup of blueberries (frozen)
- One-fourth cup of brown rice flour
- Two tbsps. of sugar
- Half tsp. of cinnamon (ground)
- Three tbsps. of butter

Method:

1. Preheat your air fryer for five minutes at 170 degrees Celsius.

2. Mix blueberries and apple in a bowl.

3. Take a bowl and mix sugar, flour, butter, and cinnamon.

4. Pour the mixture of flour over the mixture of fruits.

5. Cook the fruits in the air fryer for fifteen minutes at 170 degrees Celsius.

Kiwi Chips

Total Prep & Cooking Time: One hour

Yields: Six servings

Nutrition Facts: Calories: 110 | Protein: 2.1g | Carbs: 26.3g | Fat: 1.1g | Fiber: 1.3g

Ingredients

- One kg of kiwi
- Half tsp. of cinnamon (ground)
- One-fourth tsp. of nutmeg (ground)

Method:

1. Slice the kiwi thinly. Keep them in a bowl.

2. Sprinkle nutmeg and cinnamon from the top. Toss for mixing.

3. Preheat the air fryer at 165 degrees Celsius.

4. Cook the kiwi in the air fryer for half an hour. Make sure you shake the basket halfway.

5. Let the chips cool down in the basket for fifteen minutes.

6. Cool before serving.

Apple Crisp

Total Prep & Cooking Time: Twenty-five minutes

Yields: Two servings

Nutrition Facts: Calories: 341 | Protein: 3.9g | Carbs: 60.5g | Fat: 12.3g | Fiber: 6.9g

Ingredients

- Two apples (chopped)
- One tsp. of each
    o Lemon juice
    o Cinnamon
- Two tbsps. of brown sugar

For the topping:

- Three tbsps. of flour
- Two tbsps. of brown sugar
- Half tsp. of salt
- Four tbsps. of rolled oats
- One and a half tbsps. of butter

Method:

1. Heat your air fryer at 170 degrees Celsius. Use butter for greasing the basket.

2. Combine lemon juice, apples, cinnamon, and sugar together in a bowl.

3. Cook the mixture for fifteen minutes. Shake the basket and cook again for five minutes.

4. For the topping, mix sugar, flour, salt, butter, and oats. Use an electric mixer for mixing.

5. Scatter the topping over the cooked apples.

6. Return the basket to the air fryer. Cook again for five minutes.

Roasted Veggies

Total Prep & Cooking Time: Thirty minutes

Yields: Four servings

Nutrition Facts: Calories: 35 | Protein: 1.3g | Carbs: 3.3g | Fat: 2.6g | Fiber: 1.6g

Ingredients

- Half cup of each
  - Summer squash (diced)
  - Zucchini (diced)
  - Mushrooms (diced)
  - Cauliflower (diced)
  - Asparagus (diced)
  - Sweet red pepper (diced)
- Two tsps. of vegetable oil
- One-fourth tsp. of salt
- Half tsp. of black pepper (ground)
- One tsp. of seasoning

Method:

1. Preheat air fryer at 180 degrees Celsius.

2. Mix all the veggies, oil, pepper, seasoning, and salt in a bowl. Toss well for coating.

3. Cook the mixture of veggies in the air fryer for ten minutes.

Tempura Vegetables

Total Prep & Cooking Time: Thirty-five minutes

Yields: Four servings

Nutrition Facts: Calories: 242 | Protein: 9.2g | Carbs: 35.6g | Fat: 9.3g | Fiber: 3.7g

Ingredients

- Half cup of each
    - Flour
    - Green beans
    - Onion rings
    - Asparagus spears
    - Sweet pepper rings
    - Zucchini slices
    - Avocado wedges
- Half tsp. of each
    - Black pepper (ground)
    - Salt

- Two large eggs
- Two tbsps. of water
- One cup of panko bread crumbs
- Two tsps. of vegetable oil

Method:

1. Combine flour, pepper, and one-fourth tsp. of salt in a dish.

2. Combine water and eggs in a shallow dish.

3. Mix oil and bread crumbs in another shallow dish.

4. Sprinkle remaining salt over the veggies.

5. Dip the veggies in the mixture of flour, then in the mixture of egg, and then coat in bread crumbs.

6. Cook the veggies in the air fryer for ten minutes. Shake in between.

Eggplant Parmesan

Total Prep & Cooking Time: Thirty-five minutes

Yields: Four servings

Nutrition Facts: Calories: 370 | Protein: 24g | Carbs: 35.6g | Fat: 17g | Fiber: 8.6g

Ingredients

- Half cup of bread crumbs (Italian)
- One-fourth cup of parmesan cheese (grated)
- One tsp. of each
  - Salt
  - Italian seasoning
- Half tsp. of each
  - Basil (dried)
  - Garlic powder
  - Onion powder
  - Black pepper (ground)
- One cup of flour
- Two large eggs (beaten)
- One eggplant (sliced in round of half an inch)
- One-third cup of marinara sauce
- Eight slices of mozzarella cheese

Method:

1. Mix parmesan cheese, bread crumbs, seasoning, basil, salt, onion powder, garlic powder, and black pepper together in a mixing bowl.

2. Add flour in a shallow dish.

3. Beat the eggs in a bowl.

4. Dip the slices of eggplants in flour and then in eggs. Coat the eggplants in the mixture of bread crumbs.

5. Cook the eggplants in the air fryer for ten minutes. Flip and cook for four minutes.

6. Top the slices of eggplants with one slice of mozzarella cheese and marinara sauce.

7. Cook again for two minutes.

8. Serve hot.

French Fries

Total Prep & Cooking Time: One hour

Yields: Four servings

Nutrition Facts: Calories: 108 | Protein: 2.4g | Carbs: 17.9g | Fat: 2.1g | Fiber: 3.2g

Ingredients

- One pound of russet potatoes (peeled)
- Two tsps. of vegetable oil
- One pinch of cayenne pepper
- Half tsp. of salt

Method:

1. Cut the potatoes in half-inch slices lengthwise.

2. Soak the potatoes in water for five minutes.

3. Drain the water and soak again in boiling water for ten minutes.

4. Drain all the water. Pat dry using paper towels.

5. Add oil and cayenne pepper. Season with salt.

6. Cook the potatoes for fifteen minutes. Toss with some salt and cook again for five minutes.

Sweet and Spicy Carrots

Total Prep & Cooking Time: Thirty minutes

Yields: Two servings

Nutrition Facts: Calories: 128 | Protein: 1.2g | Carbs: 17.2g | Fat: 6g | Fiber: 4.5g

Ingredients

- One serving of cooking spray
- One tbsp. of each
  - Hot honey
  - Butter (melted)
  - Orange zest
  - Orange juice
- Half tsp. of cardamom (ground)
- Half pound of baby carrots
- One-third tsp. of black pepper and salt

Method:

1. Heat your air fryer at 200 degrees Celsius. Use a cooking spray for greasing the basket.

2. Mix honey, butter, cardamom, and orange zest in a small bowl.

3. Pour the sauce over the carrots and coat well.

4. Cook the carrots for seven twenty minutes. Toss in between.

5. Mix orange juice with the leftover sauce.

6. Serve the carrots with sauce from the top.

Baked Potatoes
Total Prep & Cooking Time: One hour and five minutes

Yields: Two servings

Nutrition Facts: Calories: 310 | Protein: 7.2g | Carbs: 61.5g | Fat: 6.3g | Fiber: 8.2g

Ingredients

- Two large potatoes
- One tbsp. of peanut oil
- Half tsp. of sea salt

Method:

1. Heat your air fryer at 200 degrees Celsius.

2. Brush the potatoes with oil. Sprinkle some salt.

3. Place the potatoes in the basket of the air fryer and cook for one hour.

4. Serve hot by dividing the potatoes from the center.

Chapter 4: Vegetarian Appetizer Recipes

You can prepare various vegetarian appetizer recipes with the help of an air fryer. Let's have a look at them.

Crunchy Brussels Sprouts
Total Prep & Cooking Time: Fifteen minutes

Yields: Two servings

Nutrition Facts: Calories: 92 | Protein: 5.2g | Carbs: 12.1g | Fat: 3.1g | Fiber: 3.2g

Ingredients

- One tsp. of avocado oil
- Half tsp. of each
  - Black pepper (ground)
  - Salt
- Ten ounces of Brussels sprouts (halved)
- One-third tsp. of balsamic vinegar

Method:

1. Heat the air fryer at 175 degrees Celsius.

2. Mix salt, pepper, and oil together in a bowl. Add the sprouts and toss.

3. Fry the Brussels sprouts in the air fryer for five minutes.

Buffalo Cauliflower
Total Prep & Cooking Time: Twenty-five minutes

Yields: Four servings

Nutrition Facts: Calories: 190 | Protein: 12.3g | Carbs: 2.3g | Fat: 12g | Fiber: 1.3g

Ingredients

- One large cauliflower
- One cup of flour
- One-fourth tsp. of each
  - Chili powder
  - Cayenne pepper
  - Paprika
- One cup of soy milk
- Two tbsps. of butter
- Two garlic cloves (minced)
- Half cup of cayenne pepper sauce
- One serving of cooking spray

Method:

1. Cut the cauliflower into small pieces. Rinse under cold water and drain.

2. Mix flour, chili powder, cayenne, and paprika in a bowl. Add the milk slowly for making a thick batter.

3. Add the pieces of cauliflower in the batter and coat well.

4. Cook the cauliflower in the air fryer for twenty minutes. Toss the cauliflower and cook again for ten minutes.

5. Take a saucepan and heat the butter in it. Add garlic and hot sauce. Boil the sauce mixture and simmer for two minutes.

6. Transfer the cauliflower to a large bowl and pour the prepared sauce over the cooked cauliflower. Toss for combining.

7. Serve hot.

Stuffed Mushrooms
Total Prep & Cooking Time: Thirty minutes

Yields: Six servings

Nutrition Facts: Calories: 42 | Protein: 3.1g | Carbs: 2.9g | Fat: 1.2g | Fiber: 2.3g

Ingredients

- Fifteen button mushrooms
- One tsp. of olive oil
- One-eighth tsp. of salt
- Half tsp. of black pepper (crushed)
- One-third tsp. of balsamic vinegar

For the filling:

- One-fourth cup of each
  - Bell pepper
  - Onion
- Two tbsps. of cilantro (chopped)
- One tbsp. of jalapeno (chopped finely)
- Half cup of mozzarella cheese (grated)
- One tsp. of coriander (ground)
- One-fourth tsp. of each
  - Paprika
  - Salt

Method:

1. Use a damp cloth for cleaning the mushrooms. Remove the stems for making the caps hollow.

2. Take a bowl and season the mushroom caps with salt, oil, balsamic vinegar, and black pepper.

3. Take another bowl and mix the ingredients for the filling.

4. Use a spoon for filling the mushroom caps. Press the filling in the mushroom using the backside of the spoon.

5. Cook the mushrooms in the air fryer for ten minutes.

6. Serve hot.

Sweet Potatoes With Baked Taquitos

Total Prep & Cooking Time: Forty-five minutes

Yields: Five servings

Nutrition Facts: Calories: 112 | Protein: 5.2g | Carbs: 19.3g | Fat: 1.6g | Fiber: 6.1g

Ingredients

- One sweet potato (cut in pieces of half an inch)
- Two tsps. of canola oil
- Half cup yellow onion (chopped)
- One garlic clove (minced)
- Two cups of black beans (rinsed)
- One chipotle pepper (chopped)
- Half tsp. of each
  - Paprika
  - Cumin

- o   Chili powder
- o   Maple syrup
- One-eighth tsp. of salt
- Three tbsps. of water
- Ten corn tortillas

Method:

1. Place the pieces of sweet potatoes in an air fryer and toss it with some oil. Cook for twelve minutes. Make sure you shake the basket in between.

2. Take a skillet and heat some oil in it. Add the garlic and onions. Sauté for five minutes until the onions are translucent.

3. Add chipotle pepper, beans, paprika, cumin, chili powder, maple syrup, and salt. Add two tbsps. of water and mix all the ingredients.

4. Add cooked potatoes and mix well.

5. Warm the corn tortillas in a skillet.

6. Put two tbsps. of beans and potato mixture in a row across the corn tortillas. Grab one end of the corn tortillas and roll them. Tuck the end under the mixture of sweet potato and beans.

7. Place the taquitos with the seam side down in the basket. Spray the taquitos with some oil. Air fry the prepared taquitos for ten minutes.

8. Serve hot.

Cauliflower Curry

Total Prep & Cooking Time: Twenty minutes

Yields: Three servings

Nutrition Facts: Calories: 160 | Protein: 5.2g | Carbs: 27.2g | Fat: 3.1g | Fiber: 5.6g

Ingredients

- One cup of vegetable stock
- Three-fourth cup of coconut milk (light)
- Two tsps. of curry powder
- One tsp. of garlic puree
- Half tsp. of turmeric
- Twelve ounces of cauliflower (cut in florets)
- One and a half cup of sweet corn kernels
- Three spring onions (sliced)
- Salt

For the topping:

- Lime wedges
- Two tbsps. of dried cranberries

Method

1. Heat your air fryer at 190 degrees Celsius.

2. Mix all ingredients in a large bowl. Combine well.

3. Transfer the cauliflower mixture to the air fryer basket.

4. Cook for fifteen minutes. Give it a mix in the middle.

Air-Fried Avocado Wedges

Total Prep & Cooking Time: Twenty minutes

Yields: Two servings

Nutrition Facts: Calories: 302 | Protein: 8.3g | Carbs: 37.2g | Fat: 17.3g | Fiber: 7.4g

Ingredients

- One-fourth cup of flour
- Half tsp. of black pepper (ground)
- One-fourth tsp. of salt
- One tsp. of water
- One ripe avocado (cut in eight slices)
- Half cup of bread crumbs
- One serving of cooking spray

Method:

1. Heat your air fryer at 200 degrees Celsius.

2. Combine pepper, salt, and flour in a bowl. Place water in another bowl.

3. Take a shallow dish and spread the bread crumbs.

4. Coat the avocado slices in flour mixture and dip it in water.

5. Coat the slices in bread crumbs. Make sure both sides are evenly coated.

6. Use cooking spray for misting the slices of avocado.

7. Cook the coated slices of avocado for four minutes. Flip the slices and cook again for three minutes.

8. Serve hot.

Crunchy Grains
Total Prep & Cooking Time: Twenty minutes

Yields: Four servings

Nutrition Facts: Calories: 71 | Protein: 5.8g | Carbs: 34.4g | Fat: 3.2g | Fiber: 7.3g

Ingredients

- Three cups of whole grains (cooked)
- Half cup of peanut oil

Method:

1. Use a paper towel for removing excess moisture from the grains.

2. Toss the grains in oil.

3. Add the coated grains in the basket of the air fryer. Cook for ten minutes. Toss the grains and cook again for five minutes.

Buffalo Chickpeas
Total Prep & Cooking Time: Thirty minutes

Yields: Two servings

Nutrition Facts: Calories: 172 | Protein: 7.2g | Carbs: 31.6g | Fat: 1.4g | Fiber: 7.4g

Ingredients

- One can of chickpeas (rinsed)
- Two tbsps. of buffalo wing sauce
- One tbsp. of ranch dressing mix (dry)

Method:

1. Heat your air fryer at 175 degrees Celsius.

2. Use paper towels for removing excess moisture from the chickpeas.

3. Transfer the chickpeas to a bowl and add the wing sauce. Add the dressing mix and combine well.

4. Cook the chickpeas in the air fryer for eight minutes. Shake the basket and cook for five minutes.

5. Let the chickpeas sit for two minutes.

6. Serve warm.

Easy Falafel
Total Prep & Cooking Time: Forty minutes

Yields: Fifteen servings

Nutrition Facts: Calories: 57.9 | Protein: 3.2g | Carbs: 8.9g | Fat: 1.4g | Fiber: 3.9g

Ingredients

- One cup of garbanzo beans
- Two cups of cilantro (remove the stems)
- Three-fourth cup of parsley (remove the stems)
- On red onion (quartered)
- One garlic clove
- Two tbsps. of chickpea flour
- One tbsp. of each
  - Cumin (ground)
  - Coriander (ground)
  - Sriracha sauce
- One tsp. of black pepper and salt (for seasoning)
- Half tsp. of each
  - Baking soda
  - Baking powder
- One serving of cooking spray

Method:

1. Soak the beans in cool water for one day. Rub the beans and remove the skin. Rinse in cold water and use paper towels for removing excess moisture.

2. Add cilantro, beans, onion, parsley, and garlic in a blender. Blend the ingredients until paste forms.

3. Transfer the blended paste to a bowl and add coriander, flour, sriracha, cumin, pepper, and salt. Mix well. Let the mixture sit for twenty minutes.

4. Add baking soda and baking powder to the mixture. Mix well.

5. Make fifteen balls from the mixture and flatten them using your hands for making patties.

6. Usea cooking spray for greasing the falafel patties.

7. Cook them for ten minutes.

8. Serve warm.

Mini Cheese and Bean Tacos

Total Prep & Cooking Time: Thirty minutes

Yields: Twelve servings

Nutrition Facts: Calories: 229 | Protein: 11.3g | Carbs: 20.2g | Fat: 10.4g | Fiber: 2.9g

Ingredients

- One can of refried beans
- One ounce of taco seasoning mix
- Twelve slices of American cheese (halved)
- Twelve tortillas
- One serving of cooking spray

Method:

1. Place the beans in a medium-sized bowl. Add the seasoning mix. Combine well.

2. Place one cheese piece in the center of each tortilla. Take one tbsp. of the bean mix and add it over the cheese. Add another cheese piece over the beans. Fold the tortillas in half. Gently press with your hands for sealing the ends.

3. Use cooking spray for spraying the tacos.

4. Cook the tacos for three minutes. Turn the tacos and cook again for three minutes

5. Serve hot.

Green Beans and Spicy Sauce

Total Prep & Cooking Time: Thirty minutes

Yields: Four servings

Nutrition Facts: Calories: 460.2 | Protein: 5.7g | Carbs: 34.4g | Fat: 30.6g | Fiber: 4.2g

Ingredients

- One cup of beer
- One and a half cup of flour
- Two tsps. of salt
- Half tsp. of black pepper (ground)
- Twelve ounces of green beans (trimmed)

For the sauce:

- One cup of ranch dressing
- Two tsps. of sriracha sauce
- One tsp. of horseradish

Method:

1. Mix flour, beer, pepper, and salt in a mixing bowl. Add the beans in the batter and coat well. Shake off extra batter.

2. Line the air fryer basket with parchment paper. Add the beans and cook for ten minutes. Shake in between.

3. Combine sriracha sauce, ranch dressing, and horseradish together in a bowl.

4. Serve the beans with sauce by the side.

Cheesy Sugar Snap Peas

Total Prep & Cooking Time: Fifteen minutes

Yields: Four servings

Nutrition Facts: Calories: 72 | Protein: 5.7g | Carbs: 8.9g | Fat: 3.3g | Fiber: 2.5g

Ingredients

- Half pound of sugar snap peas
- One tsp. of olive oil
- One-fourth cup of bread crumbs
- Half cup of parmesan cheese
- Pepper and salt (for seasoning)
- Two tbsps. of garlic (minced)

Method:

1. Remove the stem from each pea pod. Rinse the peas and drain the water.

2. Toss the peas with bread crumbs, olive oil, pepper, salt, and half of the cheese.

3. Cook the peas in the air fryer for four minutes at 175 degrees Celsius.

4. Add minced garlic and cook again for five minutes.

5. Serve the peas with remaining cheese from the top.

PART II

Chapter 1: Meal Planning 101

Sticking to a diet is something that is not the easiest in the world. When it comes down to it, we struggle to change up our diets on a whim. It might be that for the first few days, you are able to stick to it and make sure that you are only eating those foods that are better for you, but over time, you will get to a point where you feel the pressure to cave in. You might realize that sticking to your diet is difficult and think that stopping for a burger on your way home won't be too bad. You might think that figuring out lunch or dinner is too much of a hassle, or you realize that the foods that you have bought forgot a key ingredient that you needed for dinner.

The good news is, you have an easy fix. When you are able to figure out what you are making for yourself for your meals well in advance, you stop having to worry so much about the foods that you eat, what you do with them, and what you are going to reach for when it's time to eat. You will be able to change up what you are doing so that you can be certain that the meals that you are enjoying are good for you, and you won't have to worry so much about the stress that goes into it. Let's take a look at what you need to do to get started with meal planning so that you can begin to do so without having to think too much about it.

Make a Menu

First, before you do anything, make sure that you make a menu! This should be something that you do on your own, or you should sit down with your family to ask them what they prefer. If you can do this, you will be able to ensure that you've got a clear-cut plan. When you have a menu a week in advance, you save yourself time and money because you know that all of your meals will use ingredients that are similar, and you won't have to spend forever thinking about what you should make at any point in time.

Plan around Ads

When you do your menu, make it a point to glance through the weekly ads as well. Typically, you will find that there are plenty of deals that you can make use of that will save you money.

Go Meatless Once Per Week

A great thing to do that is highly recommended on the Mediterranean Diet is to have a day each week where you go meatless for dinner. By doing so, you will realize that you can actually cut costs and enjoy the foods more at the same time. It is a great way to get that additional fruit and veggie content into your day, and there are plenty of healthy options that are out there for you. You just have to commit to doing so. In the meal plans that you'll see below, you will notice that there will be a meatless day on Day 2 every week.

Use Ingredients That You Already Have On Hand

Make it a point to use ingredients that you already have on hand whenever possible. Alternatively, make sure that all of the meals that you eat during the week use very similar ingredients. When you do this, you know that you're avoiding causing any waste or losing ingredients along the way, meaning that you can save money. The good news is, on the Mediterranean diet, there are plenty of delicious meals that enjoy very similar ingredients that you can eat.

Avoid Recipes that Call for a Special Ingredient

If you're trying to avoid waste, it is a good idea for you to avoid any ingredients in meals that are not going to carry over to other meals during your weekly plan. By avoiding doing so, you can usually save yourself that money for that one ingredient that would be wasted. Alternatively, if you find that you really want that dish, try seeing if you can freeze some of it for later. When you do that, you can usually ensure that your special ingredient at least didn't go to waste.

Use Seasonal Foods

Fruits and veggies are usually cheaper when you buy them in season, and even better, when you do so, you will be enjoying a basic factor of the Mediterranean diet just by virtue of enjoying the foods when they are fresh. Fresher foods are usually tastier, and they also tend to carry more vitamins and minerals because they have not had the chance to degrade over time.

Make Use of Leftovers and Extra Portions

One of the greatest things that you can do when it comes to meal planning is to make use of your leftovers and make-ahead meals. When you do this regularly, making larger portions than you need, you can then use the extras as lunches and dinners all week long, meaning that you won't have to be constantly worrying about the food that you eat for lunch. We will use some of these in the meal plans that you will see as well.

Eat What You Enjoy

Finally, the last thing to remember with your meal plan is that you ought to be enjoying the foods that are on it at all times. When you ensure that the foods that you have on your plate are those that you actually enjoy, sticking to your meal plan doesn't become such a chore, and that means that you will be able to do better as well with your own diet. Your meal plan should be loaded up with foods that you are actually excited about enjoying. Meal planning and dieting should not be a drag—you should love every moment of it!

Chapter 2: 1 Month Meal Plan

This meal plan is designed to be used for one month to help you simplify making sure that you have delicious meals to eat without having to think. These meals are fantastic options if you don't know where to start but want to enjoy your Mediterranean diet without much hassle. For each of the five weeks included, you will get one breakfast recipe, one lunch recipe, one dinner recipe, and one snack recipe to make meal planning a breeze. So, give these recipes a try! Many of them are so delicious, you'll want to enjoy them over and over again!

Week 1: Success is no accident—you have to reach for it

Mediterranean Breakfast Sandwich

Serves: 4

Time: 20 minutes

Ingredients:

- Baby spinach (2 c.)
- Eggs (4)
- Fresh rosemary (1 Tbsp.)
- Low-fat feta cheese (4 Tbsp.)
- Multigrain sandwich thins (4)
- Olive oil (4 tsp.)
- Salt and pepper according to preference
- Tomato (1, cut into 8 slices)

Instructions:

1. Preheat your oven. This recipe works best at 375° F. Cut the sandwich things in half and brush the insides with half of your olive oil. Place the things on a baking sheet and toast for about five minutes or until the edges are lightly browned and crispy.
2. In a large skillet, heat the rest of your olive oil and the rosemary. Use medium-high heat. Crack your eggs into the skillet one at a time. Cook

until the whites have set while keeping the yolks runny. Break the yolks and flip the eggs until done.

3. Serve by placing spinach in between two sandwich thins, along with two tomato slices, an egg, and a tablespoon of feta cheese.

Greek Chicken Bowls

Serves: 4

Time: 20 minutes

Ingredients:

- Arugula (4 c.)
- Chicken breast tenders (1 lb.)
- Cucumber (1, diced)
- Curry powder (1 Tbsp.)
- Dried basil (1 tsp.)
- Garlic powder (1 tsp.)
- Kalamata olives (2 Tbsp.)
- Olive oil (1 Tbsp.)
- Pistachios (0.25 c., chopped)
- Red onion (half, sliced)
- Sunflower seeds (0.25 c.)
- Tzatziki sauce (1 c.)

Instructions:

1. In a bowl, mix in the chicken tenders, curry powder, dried basil, and garlic powder. Make sure to coat the chicken evenly.
2. Heat one tablespoon of olive oil over medium-high. Add the chicken and cook for about four minutes on each side. Remove from the pan and set aside to cool.
3. Place one cup of arugula into four bowls. Toss in the diced cucumber, onion, and kalamata olives.
4. Chop the chicken and distribute evenly between the four bowls.
5. Top with tzatziki sauce, pistachio seeds, and sunflower seeds.

Ratatouille

Serves: 8

Time: 1 hour 30 minutes

Ingredients:

- Crushed tomatoes (1 28 oz. can)
- Eggplants (2)
- Fresh basil (4 Tbsp., chopped)
- Fresh parsley (2 Tbsp., chopped)
- Fresh thyme (2 tsp.)
- Garlic cloves (4, minced and 1 tsp, minced)
- Olive oil (6 Tbsp.)
- Onion (1, diced)
- Red bell pepper (1, diced)
- Roma tomatoes (6)
- Salt and pepper to personal preference
- Yellow bell pepper (1, diced)
- Yellow squashes (2)
- Zucchinis (2)

Instructions:

1. Get your oven ready. This recipe works best at 375° F.
2. Slice the tomatoes, eggplant, squash, and zucchini into thin rounds and set them to the side.
3. Heat up two tablespoons of olive oil in an oven safe pan using medium-high heat. Sauté your onions, four cloves of garlic, and bell peppers for about ten minutes or when soft. Add in your pepper and salt along with the full can of crushed tomatoes. Add in two tablespoons of basil. Stir thoroughly.
4. Take the vegetable slices from earlier and arrange them on top of the sauce in a pattern of your choosing. For example, a slice of eggplant, followed by a slice of tomato, squash, and zucchini, then repeating. Start from the outside and work inward to the center of your pan. Sprinkle salt and pepper overtop the veggies.
5. In a bowl, toss in the remaining basil and garlic, thyme, parsley, salt, pepper, and the rest of the olive oil. Mix it all together, and spoon over the veggies.
6. Cover your pan and bake for 40 minutes. Uncover and then continue baking for another 20 minutes.

Snack Platter

Serves: 6

Time:

Ingredients:

Rosemary Almonds

- Butter (1 Tbsp.)
- Dried rosemary (2 tsp.)
- Salt (pinch)
- Whole almonds (2 c.)

Hummus

- Chickpeas (1 15 oz. can, drained and rinsed)
- Garlic clove (1, peeled)
- Lemon (half, juiced)
- Olive oil (2 Tbsp.)
- Salt and pepper according to personal preference
- Tahini (2 Tbsp.)
- Water (2 Tbsp.)

Other sides

- Bell pepper (1, sliced)
- Cucumber (1, sliced)
- Feta cheese (4 oz, cubed)
- Kalamata olives (handful, drained)
- Pepperoncini peppers (6, drained)
- Pitas (6, sliced into wedges)
- Small fresh mozzarella balls (18)
- Soppressata (6 oz.)
- Sweet cherry peppers (18)

Instructions:

1. To get started, make your rosemary almonds. Take a large skillet and place it on a burner set to medium heat. Start melting the butter in, then toss in the almonds, rosemary and a bit of salt. Toss the nuts on occasion to ensure even coating.
2. Cook the almonds for roughly ten minutes, getting them nicely toasted. Set the almonds off to the side to let them cool.
3. Now you'll set out to make the hummus. Take a blender or food processor and toss in the hummus ingredients. Blend until you get a nice, smooth paste. If you find that your paste is too thick, try blending in a bit of water until you get the desired consistency. Once you have the right consistency, taste for seasoning and adjust as necessary.
4. Pour and scrape the hummus into a bowl and drizzle in a bit of olive oil. Set it off to the side to get the rest of the platter going.
5. Grab the sweet cherry peppers and stuff them with the little balls of mozzarella. Arrange a platter in any pattern you like. If serving for a party or family, try keeping each snack in its own little segment to keep things looking neat.

Week 2: Self-belief and effort will take you to what you want to achieve

Breakfast Quesadilla

Serves: 1

Time: 10 minutes

Ingredients:

- Basil (handful)
- Eggs (2)
- Flour tortilla (1)
- Green pesto (1 tsp.)
- Mozzarella (0.25 c.)
- Salt and pepper according to personal preference
- Tomato (half, sliced)

Instructions:

1. Scramble your eggs until just a little runny. Remember, you will be cooking them further inside the quesadilla. Season with salt and pepper.
2. Take the eggs and spread over half of the tortilla.
3. Add basil, pesto, mozzarella cheese, and the slices of tomato.
4. Fold your tortilla and toast on an oiled pan. Toast until both sides are golden brown.

Greek Orzo Salad

Serves: 6

Time: 25 minutes

Ingredients:

-   Canned chickpeas (1 c., drained and rinsed)
-   Dijon mustard (0.5 tsp)
-   Dill (0.33 c., chopped)
-   Dried oregano (1 tsp)
-   English cucumber (half, diced)

- Feta cheese crumbles (0.5 c.)
- Kalamata olives (0.33 c., halved)
- Lemon (half, juice and zest)
- Mint (0.33 c., chopped)
- Olive oil (3 Tbsp.)
- Orzo pasta (1.25 c. when dry)
- Roasted red pepper (half, diced)
- Salt and pepper to taste
- Shallot (0.25 c., minced)
- White wine vinegar (2 Tbsp.)

Instructions:

1. Prepare the orzo according to the packaging details. Once the orzo is al dente, drain it and rinse until it drops to room temperature.
2. In a bowl, toss all the ingredients together until thoroughly incorporated.

One Pot Mediterranean Chicken

Serves: 4

Time: 1 hour

Ingredients:

- Chicken broth (3 c.)
- Chicken thighs (3, bone in, skin on)
- Chickpeas (1 15 oz can, drained and rinsed)
- Dried oregano (0.5 tsp.)
- Fresh parsley (2 Tbsp., chopped)

- Garlic cloves (2, minced)
- Kalamata olives (0.75 c., halved)
- Olive oil (2 tsp.)
- Onion (1, finely diced)
- Orzo pasta (8 ounces uncooked)
- Roasted peppers (0.5 c., chopped)
- Salt and pepper according to personal preference

Instructions:

1. Prepare your oven at 375°. Heat your olive oil in a large skillet over medium-high heat.
2. Season the chicken with salt and pepper on both sides. Toss the chicken into the skillet and cook for five minutes on each side, or until golden in color. Remove the chicken.
3. Take the skillet and drain most of the rendered fat, leaving about a teaspoon. Add the onion and cook for five minutes. Toss in the garlic and cook for an additional minute.
4. Now you will want to add the orzo, roasted peppers, oregano, chickpeas, and olives into the pan. Add in salt and pepper.
5. Place the thighs on top of the orzo and pour in the chicken broth.
6. Bring to a boil, then cover and place in the oven. Bake for 35 minutes or until chicken has cooked through. Top with parsley and serve.

Mediterranean Nachos

Serves: 6

Time: 10 minutes

Ingredients:

- Canned artichoke hearts (1 c., rinsed, drained, and dried)
- Canned garbanzo beans (0.75 c., rinsed, drained, and dried)
- Feta cheese (0.5 c., crumbled)
- Fresh cilantro (2 Tbsp., chopped)
- Pine nuts (2.5 Tbsp.)
- Roasted red peppers (0.5 c., dried)
- Sabra Hummus (half of their 10 oz. container)
- Tomatoes (0.5 c., chopped)
- Tortilla chips (roughly half a bag)

Instructions:

1. Get your oven ready by setting it to 375°F. In a baking pan, layer the tortilla chips, and spread hummus over them evenly. Top with garbanzo beans, red peppers, artichoke hearts, feta cheese, and pine nuts.
2. Bake for about five minutes or until warmed through. Remove the baking pan and top the nachos with fresh cilantro and tomatoes. Serve and enjoy.

Week 3: The harder you work, the greater the success

Breakfast Tostadas

Serves: 4

Time: 15 minutes

Ingredients:

- Beaten eggs (8)
- Cucumber (0.5 c., seeded and chopped)
- Feta (0.25 c., crumbled)
- Garlic powder (0.5 tsp)
- Green onions (0.5 c., chopped)
- Oregano (0.5 tsp)
- Red Pepper (0.5 c., diced)
- Roasted red pepper hummus (0.5 c.)
- Skim milk (0.5 c.)
- Tomatoes (0.5 c., diced)
- Tostadas (4)

Instructions:

1. In a large skillet, cook the red pepper for two minutes on medium heat until softened. Toss in the eggs, garlic powder, milk, oregano, and green onions. Stir constantly until the egg whites have set.
2. Top the tostadas with hummus, egg mixture, cucumber, feta, and tomatoes.

Roasted Vegetable Bowl

Serves: 2

Time: 45 minutes

Ingredients:

- Crushed red pepper flakes (a pinch)
- Fresh parsley (1 Tbsp., chopped)
- Kalamata olives (0.25 c.)
- Kale (1 c., ribboned)
- Lemon juice (1 Tbsp.)
- Marinated artichoke hearts (0.25 c., drained and chopped)
- Nutritional yeast (1 Tbsp.)
- Olive oil (1 Tbsp., then enough to drizzle)
- Salt and pepper to taste
- Spaghetti squash (half, seeds removed)
- Sun-dried tomatoes (2 Tbsp., chopped)
- Walnuts (0.25 c., chopped)

Instructions:

1. Get your oven ready by setting it to 400° F. Take a baking sheet and blanket it with parchment paper.
2. Take the squash half and place it on the parchment paper. Drizzle olive oil over the side that is cut, and season with salt and pepper. Turn it over so it is facing cut side down and bake for 40 minutes. It is ready when it is soft.
3. Remove the squash shell, and season with a bit more salt and pepper.
4. Stack the kale, artichoke hearts, walnuts, sun-dried tomatoes, and kalamata olives on the squash.
5. Squeeze the lemon juice over and drizzle olive oil. Finish with chopped parsley and a bit of crushed red pepper flakes.

Mediterranean Chicken

Serves: 4

Time: 40 minutes

Ingredients:

- Chicken breasts (1 lb., boneless, skinless)
- Chives (2 Tbsp., chopped)
- Feta cheese (0.25 c., crumbled)
- Garlic (1 tsp., minced)
- Italian seasoning (1 tsp.)
- Lemon juice (2 Tbsp.)
- Olive oil (2 Tbsp., and 1 Tbsp.)
- Salt and pepper according to personal preference
- Tomatoes (1 c., diced)

Instructions:

1. Pour in two tablespoons of olive oil, the lemon juice, salt, pepper, garlic, and Italian seasoning in a resealable plastic bag. Add in the chicken, seal and shake to coat the chicken.
2. Allow the chicken to marinate for at least 30 minutes in the refrigerator.
3. Heat the rest of the olive oil in a pan over medium heat.
4. Place the chicken on the pan and cook for five minutes on each side, or until cooked through.
5. In a bowl, mix the tomatoes, chives, and feta cheese. Season with salt and pepper.
6. When serving, spoon the tomato mixture on top of the chicken.

Baked Phyllo Chips

Serves: 2

Time: 10 minutes

Ingredients:

- Grated cheese (your choice)
- Olive oil (enough to brush with)
- Phyllo sheets (4)
- Salt and pepper according to personal preference

Instructions:

1. Get your oven ready by setting it to 350° F. Brush olive oil over a phyllo sheet generously. Sprinkle grated cheese and your seasoning on top.
2. Grab a second sheet of your phyllo and place it on top of the first one. Again, brush with olive oil and sprinkle cheese and seasoning on top.
3. Repeat this process with the remaining sheets of phyllo. Top the stack with cheese and seasoning.
4. Once complete, cut the stack of phyllo into bite-sized rectangles. A pizza cutter may be helpful here.
5. Grab a baking sheet and blanket it with some parchment paper. Take your phyllo rectangles and place them on the parchment paper.
6. Bake in the oven for about seven minutes or until they reach a golden color.
7. Remove them from the oven and allow them to cool before serving.

Week 4: You don't need perfection—you need effort

Mini Omelets

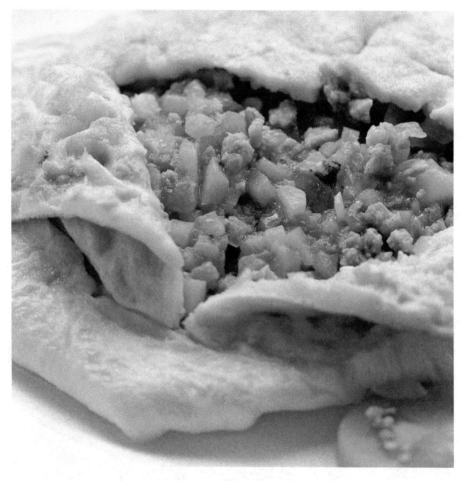

Serves: 8

Time: 40 minutes

Ingredients:

- Cheddar cheese (0.25 c., shredded)
- Eggs (8)
- Half and half (0.5 c.)
- Olive oil (2 tsps.)
- Salt and pepper according to personal preference
- Spinach (1 c., chopped)

Instructions:

1. Get your oven ready by setting it to 350° F. Prepare a muffin pan or ramekins by greasing them with olive oil.
2. In a bowl, beat the eggs and dairy until you have a fluffy consistency.
3. Stir in the cheese and your seasonings. Pour in the spinach and continue beating the eggs.
4. Pour the egg mixture into your ramekins or muffin pan.
5. Bake the omelets until they have set, which should be roughly 25 minutes. Remove them from the oven and allow them to cool before serving.

Basil Shrimp Salad

Serves: 2

Time: 40 minutes

Ingredients:

- Dried basil (1 tsp.)
- Lemon juice (1 Tbsp.)
- Olive oil (1 tsp.)
- Romaine lettuce (2 c.)
- Shrimp (12 medium or 8 large)
- White wine vinegar (0.25 c.)

Instructions:

1. Whisk together the white wine vinegar, olive oil, lemon juice, and basil. Stick your shrimp in the marinade for half an hour.
2. Take the marinade and shrimp and cook in a skillet over medium heat until cooked through.
3. Allow the shrimp to cool along with the juice and pour into a bowl. Toss in the romaine lettuce and mix well to get the flavor thoroughly infused in the salad. Serve.

Mediterranean Flounder

Serves: 4

Time: 40 minutes

Ingredients:

- Capers (0.25 c.)
- Diced tomatoes (1 can)
- Flounder fillets (1 lb.)
- Fresh basil (12 leaves, chopped)
- Fresh parmesan cheese (3 Tbsp., grated)
- Garlic cloves (2, chopped)
- Italian seasoning (a pinch)
- Kalamata olives (0.5 c., pitted and chopped)
- Lemon juice (1 tsp.)
- Red onion (half, chopped)
- White wine (0.25 c.)

Instructions:

1. Set your oven to 425° F. Take a skillet and pour in enough olive oil to sauté the onion until soft. Cook on medium-high heat.
2. Toss in the garlic, Italian seasoning, and tomatoes. Cook for an additional five minutes.
3. Pour in the wine, capers, olives, lemon juice, and only half of the basil you chopped.
4. Reduce the heat to low and stir in the parmesan cheese. Simmer for ten minutes or until the sauce has thickened.
5. Place the flounder fillets in a baking pan and pour the sauce over top. Sprinkle the remaining basil on top and bake for 12 minutes.

Nutty Energy Bites

Serves: 10

Time: 10 minutes

Ingredients:

- Dried dates (1 c., pitted)
- Almonds (0.5 c.)
- Pine nuts (0.25 c.)

- Flaxseeds (1 Tbsp., milled)
  Porridge oats (2 Tbsp.)
- Pistachios (0.25 c., coarsely ground)

Instructions:

1. Take the dates, pine nuts, milled flaxseeds, almonds, and porridge oats and pour them into a food processor or blender. Mix until thoroughly incorporated.
2. Using a tablespoon, scoop the mixture and roll it between your hands until you have a small, bite-sized ball. Do this until you have used the entirety of the dough. This recipe should be enough for about ten.
3. On a plate, sprinkle your ground pistachios. Take the energy balls and roll them on the pistachio grounds, making sure to coat them evenly. Serve or store in the refrigerator.

Week 5: Transformation Happens One Day at a Time

Mediterranean Breakfast Bowl

Serves: 1

Time: 25 minutes

Ingredients:

- Artichoke hearts (0.25 c., chopped)
- Baby arugula (2 c.)
- Capers (1 Tbsp.)
- Egg (1)

95

- Feta (2 Tbsp., crumbled)
- Garlic (0.25 tsp)
- Kalamata olives (5, chopped)
- Lemon thyme (1 Tbsp., chopped)
- Olive oil (0.5 Tbsp.)
- Pepper (0.25 tsp)
- Sun-dried tomatoes (2 Tbsp., chopped)
- Sweet potato (1 c., cubed)

Instructions:

1. Take your olive oil and, when hot, pan fry your sweet potatoes for 5-10 minutes until they have softened. Then, sprinkle on the seasonings.
2. Place arugula into a bowl, then top with potatoes, then everything but the egg.
3. Prepare the egg to your liking and serve.

Chicken Shawarma Pita Pockets

Serves: 6

Time: 40 minutes

Ingredients:

- Cayenne (0.5 tsp)
- Chicken thighs (8, boneless, skinless, bite-sized pieces)
- Cloves (0.5 tsp, ground)
- Garlic powder (0.75 Tbsp.)
- Ground cumin (0.75 Tbsp.)
- Lemon juice (1 lemon)
- Olive oil (0.33 c.)
- Onion (1, sliced thinly)
- Paprika (0.75 Tbsp.)
- Salt
- Turmeric powder (0.75 Tbsp.)

To serve:

- Pita pockets (6)
- Tzatziki sauce
- Arugula
- Diced tomatoes
- Diced onions
- Sliced Kalamata olives

Instructions:

1. Combine all spices. Then, place all chicken, already diced, into the bowl. Coat well, then toss in onions, lemon juice, and oil. Mix well and let marinade for at least 3 hours, or overnight.
2. Preheat the oven to 425 F. Allow chicken to sit at room temperature a few minutes. Then, spread it on an oiled sheet pan. Roast for 30 minutes.
3. To serve, fill up a pita pocket with tzatziki, chicken, arugula, and any toppings you prefer. Enjoy.

Turkey Mediterranean Casserole

Serves: 6

Time: 35 minutes

Ingredients:

- Fusilli pasta (0.5 lbs.)
- Turkey (1.5 c., chopped)
- Sun dried tomatoes (2 Tbsp., drained)
- Canned artichokes (7 oz., drained)
- Kalamata olives (3.5 oz., drained and chopped)
- Parsley (0.5 Tbsp., chopped and fresh)
- Basil (1 T, fresh)
- Salt and pepper to taste
- Marinara sauce (1 c.)
- Black chopped olives (2 oz., drained)
- Mozzarella cheese (1.5 c., shredded)

Instructions:

1. Warm your oven to 350 F. Prepare your pasta according to the directions, drain, and place into a bowl. Prepare your basil, parsley, olives, tomatoes, artichokes, and other ingredients.
2. Mix together the pasta with the turkey, tomatoes, olives, artichokes, herbs, seasoning, and marinara sauce. Give it a good mix to incorporate all of the ingredients evenly.
3. Take a 9x13 oven-safe dish and layer in the first half of your pasta mixture. Then, sprinkle on half of your mozzarella cheese. Top with the rest of the pasta, then sprinkle on the chopped black olives as well. Spread the rest of the shredded cheese on top, then bake it for 20-25 minutes. It is done when the cheese is all bubbly and the casserole is hot.

Heirloom Tomato and Cucumber Toast

Serves: 2

Time: 5 minutes

Ingredients:

- Heirloom tomato (1, diced)
- Persian cucumber (1, diced)
- Extra virgin olive oil (1 tsp)
- Oregano (a pinch, dried)
- Kosher salt and pepper
- Whipped cream cheese (2 tsp)
- Whole grain bread (2 pieces)
- Balsamic glaze (1 tsp)

Instructions:

4. Combine the tomato, cucumber, oil, and all seasonings together.
5. Spread cheese across bread, then top with mixture, followed by balsamic glaze.

Chapter 3: Maintaining Your Diet

Sticking to a diet can be tough. You could see that other people are having some great food and wish that you could enjoy it too. You might realize that you miss the foods that you used to eat and feel like it's a drag to not be able to enjoy them. When you are able to enjoy the foods that you are eating, sticking to your diet is far easier. However, that doesn't mean that you won't miss those old foods sometimes. Thankfully, the Mediterranean diet is not a very restrictive one—you are able to enjoy foods in moderation that would otherwise not be allowed, and because of that, you can take the slice of cake at the work party, or you can choose to pick up a coffee for yourself every now and then. When you do this, you're not doing anything wrong, so long as you enjoy food in moderation.

Within this chapter, we are going to take a look at several tips that you can use that will help you with maintaining your diet so that you will be able to stick to it, even when you feel like things are getting difficult. Think of this as your guide to avoiding giving in entirely—this will help you to do the best thing for yourself so that you can know that you are healthy. Now, let's get started.

Find Your Motivation

First, if you want to keep yourself on your diet, one of the best things that you can do is make sure that you find and stick to your motivation. Make sure that you know what it is in life that is motivating you. Are you losing weight because a doctor told you to? Fair enough—but how do you make that personal and about yourself? Maybe instead of looking at it as a purely health-related choice, look at it as something that you are doing because of yourself. Maybe you are eating better so that you are able to watch your children graduate or so that you can run after them at the park and stay healthy, even when it is hard to do so.

Remind Yourself Why You are Eating Healthily

When you find that you are struggling to eat healthily, remind yourself of why you are doing it in the first place. When you do this enough, you will begin to resist the urges easier than ever. Make it a point to tell yourself not to eat something a certain way. Take the time to remind yourself that you don't need to order that greasy pizza—you are eating better foods because you want to be there for your children or grandchildren.

Reminding yourself of your motivation is a great way to overcome those cravings that you may have at any point in time. The cravings that you have are usually strong and compelling, but if you learn to overcome them, you realize that they weren't actually as powerful as you thought they were. Defeat the cravings. Learn to tell yourself that they are not actually able to control you. Tell yourself that you can do better with yourself.

Eat Slowly

Now, on the Mediterranean diet, you should already be eating your meals with other people anyway. You should be taking the time to enjoy those meals while talking to other people and ensuring that you get that connection with them, and in doing so, you realize that you are able to do better. You realize that you are able to keep yourself under control longer, and that is a great way to defend and protect yourself from overeating.

When you eat slowly, you can get the same effect. Eating slowly means that you will have longer for your brain to realize that you should be eating less. When you are able to trigger that sensation of satiety because you were eating slowly, you end up eating fewer calories by default, and that matters immensely.

Keep Yourself Accountable

Don't forget that, ultimately, your diet is something that you must control on your own. Keep yourself accountable by making sure that you show other people what you are doing. If you are trying to lose weight, let them know, and tell them how you plan to do so. When you do this, you are able to remind yourself that other people know what you are doing and why—this is a great way to foster that sense of accountability because you will feel like you have to actually follow through, or you will be embarrassed by having to admit fault. You could also make accountability to yourself as well. When you do this, you are able to remind yourself that your diet is your own. Using apps to track your food and caloric intake is just one way that you can do this.

Remember Your Moderation

While it can be difficult to face a diet where you feel like you can't actually enjoy the foods that you would like to eat, the truth is that on the Mediterranean diet, you are totally okay to eat those foods that you like or miss if you do so in moderation. There is nothing that is absolutely forbidden on the Mediterranean diet—there are just foods that you should be restricting regularly. However, that doesn't mean that you can't have a treat every now and then.

Remembering to live in moderation will help you from feeling like you have to cheat or give up as well. When you are able to enjoy your diet and still enjoy the times where you want to enjoy your treats, you realize that there is actually a happy medium between sticking to the diet and deciding to quit entirely.

Identify the Difference between Hunger and Craving

Another great way to help yourself stick to your diet is to recognize that there is a very real difference between actually being hungry and just craving something to eat. In general, cravings are felt in the mouth—when you feel like you are salivating or like you need to eat something, but it is entirely in your head and mouth, you know that you have a craving. When you are truly hungry, you feel an emptiness in your stomach—you are able to know because your abdomen is where the motivation is coming from.

Being able to tell when you have a craving and when you are genuinely hungry, you can usually avoid eating extra calories that you didn't actually need. This is major—if you don't want to overeat, you need to know when your body actually needs something and when it just wants something. And if you find that you just want something, that's okay too—just find a way to move on from it. If you want to indulge a bit here and there, there's no harm in that!

Stick to the Meal Plan

When it comes to sticking to a diet, one of the easiest and most straightforward ways to do so is to just stick to your meal plan that you set up. You have it there for a reason—it is there for you to fall back on, and the sooner that you are willing to accept that, recognizing that ultimately, you can stay on track when you don't have to think about things too much, the better you will do. You will be able to succeed on your diet because you will know that you have those tools in place to protect you—they will be lined up to ensure that your diet is able to provide you with everything that you need and they will also be there so that you can know that you are on the right track.

Drink Plenty of Water

Another key to keeping yourself on track with your diet is to make sure that you drink plenty of water throughout the day. Oftentimes, we mistake our thirst with hunger and eat instead. Of course, if you're thirsty, food isn't going to really fix your problem, and you will end up continuing to mix up the sensation as you try to move past it. The more you eat, the thirstier you will get until you realize that you're full but still feeling "hungry." By drinking plenty of water any time that you think that you might want to eat, you will be able to keep yourself hydrated, and in addition, you will prevent yourself from unintentionally eating too much.

Eat Several Times Per Day

One of the best ways to keep yourself on track with your diet is to make sure that you are regularly eating. By eating throughout the day, making sure that you keep yourself full, it is easier to keep yourself strong enough to resist giving in to cravings or anything else. When you do this regularly, you will discover that you can actually keep away much of your cravings so that you are more successful in managing your diet.

Eating several times per day often involves small meals and snacks if you prefer to do so. Some people don't like doing this, but if you find that you're one of those people who will do well on a diet when you are never actually hungry enough to get desperate enough to break it, you will probably be just fine.

Fill Up on Protein

Another great way to protect yourself from giving in and caving on your diet is to make sure that you fill up on protein. Whether it comes from an animal or plant source, make sure that every time you eat, you have some sort of tangible protein source. This is the best way to keep yourself on track because protein keeps you fuller for longer. When you eat something that's loaded up with protein, you don't feel the need to eat as much later on. The protein is usually very dense, and that means that you get to resist feeling hungry for longer than you thought that you would.

Some easy proteins come from nuts—but make sure that you are mindful that you do not end up overeating during this process—you might unintentionally end up eating too many without realizing it. While you should be eating proteins regularly, make sure that you are mindful of calorie content as well!

Keep Only Healthy Foods

A common mistake that people make while dieting is that they end up caving when they realize that their home is filled up with foods that they shouldn't be eating. Perhaps you are the only person in your home that is attempting to diet. In this case, you may end up running into a situation where you have all sorts of non-compliant foods on hand. You might have chips for your kids or snacks that your partner likes to eat on hand. You may feel like it is difficult for you to stay firm when you have that to consider, and that means that you end up stuck in temptation.

One of the best ways to prevent this is to either cut all of the unhealthy junk out of your home entirely or make sure that you keep the off-limits foods in specific places so that you don't have to look at it and see it tempting you every time that you go to get a snack for yourself. By trying to keep yourself limited to just healthy foods, you will be healthier, and you will make better decisions.

Eat Breakfast Daily

Finally, make sure that breakfast is non-negotiable. Make sure that you enjoy it every single day, even if you're busy. This is where those make-ahead meals can come in handy; by knowing that you have to keep to a meal plan and knowing that you already have the food on hand, you can keep yourself fed. Breakfast sets you up for success or failure—if you want to truly succeed on your diet, you must make sure that you are willing to eat those healthier foods as much as possible, and you must get started on the right foot. Enjoy those foods first thing every day. Eat so that you are not ravenous when you finally do decide that it is time to sit down and find something to eat. Even if you just have a smoothie or something quick to eat as you go, having breakfast will help you to persevere.

PART III

Chapter 1: The Fundamentals of a Low Sugar Diet

for Diabetics

For people with diabetes, eating can be quite a challenge. After all, it's not easy dealing with the various recommendations made by doctors. The fact is that the following recommended guidelines are essential to keeping your diabetes in check.

You see, it's important to ensure that your blood sugar levels remain in check. One of the easiest and most effective ways to do this is by keeping your sugar and carb intake as low as possible. So, let's take a look at how this occurs when you go on the low-sugar and low-carb, diabetic diet.

Firstly, when you consume carbs and sugars, these are converted into glucose in the bloodstream as the liver metabolizes them. Since carbs are used as a source of energy, the body needs to secrete insulin from the pancreas in order to break down glucose and send it into the cells as functional energy. Then, the body mixes oxygen to create ATP. This is the source of energy that helps you power your body's entire system.

All is good until there is an excess of glucose in the body. When this occurs, the body stores excess glucose as fat. However, there comes a point where the body just can't keep up. This is where insulin resistance happens. In a nutshell, your cells simply stop accepting any more glucose as there is simply too much glucose in the bloodstream. These are the spikes in blood sugar levels.

This is where the low-carb, low-sugar diet makes a huge difference in your overall health management plan. The rationale is that when you restrict the number of carbs and sugar that you consume, you are basically giving your body the chance to process what's already in the bloodstream and in storage. So, you are creating a deficit that forces the body to use up what it's already stored.

This is how you can get your blood sugar levels in check.

In a manner of speaking, what you are doing is giving your body a break. Therefore, the body has a chance to catch up. When your body eventually catches up, you end up reducing your overall blood sugar levels. In addition, medication is much more effective as there are fewer carbs and glucose to process.

At first, it can be a bit of a psychological shock to think that you have to go on a low-carb, low-sugar diet. In fact, most people think they have to live on lettuce for the rest of their lives. What you will find is that this diet embraces a large number of foods that are very low in carbs and sugar. As a result, you can eat healthy and tasty at the same time.

However, the secret is knowing which foods promote low blood sugar levels. When you discover these foods, you'll find that keeping your diabetes in check doesn't have to be tough. You can still enjoy delicious foods with zero guilt.

Now that's a plan!

Chapter 2: Benefits of a Low Sugar Diet for Diabetics

The low-sugar, low-carb diet is filled with a number of benefits that diabetics can obtain. The best part is that you don't need to wait for an extended period of time to see the benefits. In fact, you can see benefits within a few days of trying out the diet. This is what makes the diet itself so encouraging.

So, here is a list of five benefits you can expect when going on the low-sugar diet.

1. Reduction in blood sugar levels

Naturally, this is the most immediate benefit of this diet. As mentioned earlier, when you reduce the amount of carbs and sugar, your body will begin to use up what's already stored in the system. This is why you can begin to see a reduction in your blood sugar levels within a few days. Over time, your blood sugar levels will begin to normalize. So, the diet, along with medication, will prove to be quite effective.

2. Weight loss

Another benefit is weight loss. Since the body converts glucose into fat when it's stored, a reduction in your carb and sugar consumption will force your body to convert stored fat into energy. This is why folks who go on the low-carb diet begin to see weight loss after a few weeks. While this result isn't immediate, it is almost certain that you'll see weight loss, especially if you are overweight.

3. Increased levels of energy

One of the symptoms that accompany diabetes is low levels of energy. This is due to the imbalance that occurs in the metabolism. Since the metabolism cannot keep up with the amount of carbs and sugar in the bloodstream, it does not produce energy as efficiently as it could. As a result, there are lower levels of energy. When you essentially force your body to process stored up fat, your metabolism becomes more efficient in producing energy. The end result is a boost in energy levels. So, don't be surprised if you find at you feel more energetic after a few days.

4. Hormonal regulation

Hormones tend to go out of whack when there are increased levels of blood sugar. For instance, insulin is the first hormone that goes haywire. However, other hormones are affected as well, such as cortisol (it is associated with weight gain) or epinephrine (used to breakdown and release nutrients in the blood). These hormones tend to work inefficiently when there is a high level of blood sugar. As a result, you may not be getting the most nutrition out of the foods you eat.

5. Improved cognitive function

Sugar, in general, works like a fuel in your body. So, when you consume a large amount of sugar, you get the rush that can power you through a given time period. However, sugar is a very poor fuel as your brain burns right through it. The end result is a severe crash afterward. Over time, your brain builds up "gunk." This gunk limits the brain's capabilities. As such, when you replace sugar with other types of fuels, such as vegetable-based carbs, then your brain produces energy more effectively. It's like putting diesel into an unleaded engine. Sure, the car will run, but it will run poorly. This is why many folks on the low-sugar diet report improved cognitive abilities, thereby reducing the phenomenon known as "brain fog."

With these benefits, you can't go wrong with the low-sugar diet!

Chapter 3: Savory Recipe Ideas

Savory Idea #1: Tangy Cabbage Treat
Number of people served: 4
Time you'll need: 33 to 37 minutes

Calories: 253

Fats: 22.8 g
Proteins: 7.9 g
Carbs: 4.7 g

What you'll require:

- Jalapeno Peppers (two, chopped)
- Cabbage (one Head)
- Pepper & salt (as preferred)
- Onion (one, chopped)
- Bacon (six, strips)

What you need to do:

1. Firstly, cook bacon as per the directions on the pack. While you allow the bacon to reach its optimal point, ready cabbage, and onions by chopping into smaller bite-sized morsels.
2. Once the bacon has been prepared to your preference, take it out of the pan and toss the onion and cabbage in. Please ensure to mix up everything with the leftover grease from the bacon while simmering in low fire.
3. Next, get the jalapenos ready by cutting up into pieces as small as you like. Feel free to throw in with the other elements.
4. After the vegetables have reached their optimal point, take the crispy bacon and crumble over the entire mix. Add pepper & salt, along with any other low-carb or low-sugar spices.
5. Lastly, toss everything around until the entire mix is thoroughly even. Serve and enjoy!

Number of people served: 6
Time you'll need: 11 to 14 minutes

Calories: 21.8
Fats: 3.7 g
Proteins: 4.3 g
Carbs: 1.8 g

What you'll require:

- Bell Pepper (75 g, Chopped)
- Cucumber (45 g, Chopped)
- Spinach (225 g, Chopped)
- Tomato (75 g, Chopped)
- Eggs (three)
- Salt (as preferred)

What you need to do:

1. To get started, set up oven to 180 degrees Celsius along with a muffin tray. The smaller trays are better as they allow for smaller portions if you wish.
2. Next, use a mixing container and place eggs (cracked) inside. Whisk briskly until they are thoroughly mixed.
3. Now, coat trays with your choice of grease (for instance, non-stick spray). Please ensure to leave some extra for the vegetables (chopped)
4. Then, place eggs in the spaces in the tray and toss in vegetables are per your preference. Please make sure to stir so that the mix is distributed evenly. Then, place in the heat for roughly 11 to 14 minutes.
5. Lastly, make sure to check the mixture is cooked all the way through. Serve as a breakfast treat or yummy snack.

Savory Idea #3: Yummy Chicken Dee-light

Number of people served: 2
Time you'll need: 35 to 40 minutes

Calories: 794.7
Fats: 39.1 g
Proteins: 44.2 g
Carbs: 3.3 g

What you'll require:

- Rosemary Leaves (10 g)

- Pepper & salt (as preferred)
- Garlic (cloves, six, minced)
- Chicken Breast (455 g boneless & skinless)
- Cheddar Cheese (70 g, shredded)
- Butter (55 g)

What you need to do:

1. Firstly, set up your oven to a temperature of approximately 190 degrees Celsius. While the oven gain temperature, prepare a tray with grease (your choice).
2. Next, add seasoning to chicken to your liking.
3. Then, begin to prepare garlic butter. Take pan or skillet and set to medium fire on the range. Once the butter has thoroughly melted, toss in garlic and let cook for roughly five to six minutes. Once this time has passed, garlic should be brownish, but make sure it is not burnt. Now, cover chicken with this butter & garlic mix.
4. Once this mix is prepared, set into the oven for about ½ an hour. Make sure to check the chicken so that it is fully cooked all the way through to the center. Once this has been achieved, add cheese as a topping. Allow to melt.
5. Serve by adding some more butter & garlic mix on top. Enjoy!

Savory Idea #4: Low-carb Fried Chicken Surprise

Number of people served: 6
Time you'll need: 33 minutes

Calories: 768
Fats: 54.1 g
Proteins: 59.2 g
Carbs: 1.9 g

What you'll require:

- Pork (rinds, 85 g)
- Pepper & salt (as preferred)
- Lard (according to need)
- Egg (one)
- Chicken (thighs, six)

What you need to do:

1. First, heat up iron pan or skillet on a range top. Then, place eggs in a mixing container for whisking.
2. Next, prepare rinds by crumbling. Upon completion, coat chicken pieces with egg (you can use a brush or dip) and season as per your liking with salt & pepper.
3. Now, take covered chicken pieces and roll over in the rind crumbs. Do this for every piece.
4. After, add in about half an inch of lard (or cooking oil) into pan or skillet. Wait until it reaches the boiling point. Then, place chicken pieces into the fire. Leave for about four to six minutes on each side. Please make sure they are cooked all the way through.
5. Please ensure to turn chicken around at least twice to ensure proper cooking. Serve with a side of crispy veggies or veggie chips.

Savory Idea #5: Low-Sugar Beef Explosion
Number of people served: 4
Time you'll need: one hour

Calories: 331
Fats: 26.7 g
Proteins: 18.7 g
Carbs: 2.1 g

What you'll require:

- Garlic (cloves, two, chopped)
- Coconut grounds (55 g)
- Onions (green, three)
- Coconut Oil (45 g)
- Ginger (10 g, grated)
- Steak (Flat-iron, 455 g)

What you need to do:

1. First, get steak ready by cutting it up into long, thin slices. Upon completion, place into a large freezer bag so that you can add ginger, coconut grounds, and garlic. Then, place into refrigeration so it can marinate for about one hour's time.
2. Next, put a pan or skillet to heat. Add oil for the meat. Heat up for about three to four minutes until it is at boiling point. Then, toss in steak and let sit until thoroughly cooked. This should take about five to seven minutes.
3. After, add in onions (green) to give the flavor a kick. Let everything sit for a minute or two until the texture is as per your liking.
4. Lastly, take some of the marinade from the freezer bag and add in right before turning off the fire. This will add an extra kick. Serve over zucchini pasta or low-carb couscous.

Savory Idea #6: Tangy Pork Extravaganza

Number of people served: 4
Time you'll need: 34 to 37 minutes

Calories: 466.1
Fats: 32.3 g
Proteins: 47.2 g
Carbs: 2.7 g

What you'll require:

- Stock (chicken, 55 g)
- Pepper (7.5 g)
- Pork (chops, four)
- Milk (202 g)
- Coriander (9 g)

- Thyme (dried, 14.5 g)
- Garlic (cloves, two, minced)
- Butter (47 g)
- Salt (14.5 g)
- Oregano (dried, 14.5 g)

What you need to do:

1. First, get chops ready by placing them on a baking sheet. Sprinkle with pepper & salt to season. Please ensure that seasoning is evenly distributed to guarantee flavor. Let sit for one hour. Once time has passed, carefully rinse chops of excess fluid.
2. Next, set the pan to high heat on range top. Place garlic & butter to stir. Once the garlic is fully transparent, the time has come to add in chops on top.
3. Once chops are placed, cook them through for roughly four to six minutes on both sides. Then, let simmer for another minute, or so, to enable flavors to combine. Remove and set aside.
4. Then, on low fire, throw in stock (chicken), and some milk. Scrape the little leftover bits from the chops. Upon completion, toss oregano, coriander, and thyme in. Please ensure you are only simmering and not boiling the sauce.
5. Lastly, as the sauce thickens, turn the heat off and toss chops back into skillet. Combine all elements and add more pepper & salt if desired. Serve with veggies or a fresh salad.

Savory Idea #7: Filet & Cheese Supreme
Number of people served: 3 or 4
Time you'll need: 31 to 36 minutes

Calories: 211
Fats: 17.4 g
Proteins: 11.9 g
Carbs: 2.25 g

What you'll require:

- Paprika (4.5 g)
- Fish Fillet (225 g)
- Parsley (flakes, 7.5 g)
- Pepper (black, 4.5 g)
- Oil (Olive, 18.5 g)
- Cheese (Parmesan, 45 g)

What you need to do:

1. First, heat up the oven to approximately 180 degrees Celsius.
2. Now, get mixing container for the pepper (black), paprika, cheese (Parmesan), and parsley.
3. Then, cover filets with the spice mix. Add oil (olive) and then rollup the mixture ensuring an even coating.
4. Once the fish is ready, set the filets on to tray and place it into the oven for roughly fourteen to seventeen minutes.
5. Lastly, double-check fish is thoroughly cooked and place cheese on top to create a crust. Let sit for a few moments, until cheese is crispy, remove, and serve. Enjoy with veggies or low-carb brown rice.

Savory Idea #8: Quick and Easy Low-carb Chips
Number of people served: 4
Time you'll need: 28 to 34 minutes

Calories: 91.7
Fats: 8.1 g
Proteins: 3.2 g
Carbs: 2.8 g

What you'll require:

- Salt (as preferred)
- Pepper (as preferred)
- Bacon (slices, eight)
- Oil (Olive, 18.5 g)

What you need to do:

1. First, set up an oven to approximately 180 degrees Celsius.
2. Next, grease a tray with oil (olive) or your choice of grease. Then, break up the bacon into small, bite-sized pieces.
3. After, season with pepper & salt as per your taste.
4. Then, throw into the oven for roughly eighteen to twenty-one minutes. Remove and let cool.
5. Once cool to touch, take bits and put into a skillet, or pan, over medium fire. This process usually takes about four to six minutes. Remove from fire and serve as chips. You can serve with a low-fat, low-carb dip as an appetizer!

Savory Idea #9: Unbelievably Low-carb South Treat

Number of people served: 3 to 4
Time you'll need: 29 to 32 minutes

Calories: 288
Fats: 22.3 g
Proteins: 18.9 g
Carbs: 2.7 g

What you'll require:

- Turkey Breast (roasted, 225 g, chopped)
- Cheese (Parmesan, 75 g)

- Cheddar Cheese (shredded, 225 g)
- White Cheddar Cheese (shredded, 225 g)

What you need to do:

1. First, set up an oven to approximately 180 degrees Celsius.
2. Next, take a mixing container and combine all cheeses. You can whisk or use an electric mixer. Then, take a spoonful of the mix and place onto baking sheet in a clump. Lay down as you would with cookies. Space clumps about one inch apart.
3. Upon filling sheet, throw into over for roughly seven to eight minutes. Please ensure that chips do not get burned. Chips are cooked thoroughly when edges turn light to a golden brown. Then, remove and let cool all the way.
4. Lastly, chop up turkey breast and serve chips with a low-sugar dip. Serve as a snack or entrée.

Savory Idea #10: Low-sugar Italian Snack Option
Number of people served: 4 to 6
Time you'll need: About 22 minutes

Calories: 226
Fats: 23.7 g
Proteins: 18.4 g
Carbs: 5.7 g

What you'll require:

- Mozzarella Cheese (shredded, 225 g)
- Pepper (as preferred)
- Seasoning (Italian, 14.5 g)
- Pepperoni (115 g, chopped)
- Garlic (powder, 8.5 g)
- Salt (as preferred)
- Additional choice: Marinara Sauce for Dipping

What you need to do:

1. First, set up an oven to approximately 180 degrees Celsius.
2. Next, take a small muffin tray and coat with spray (cooking). Leave to one side.
3. Then, in a mixing container, combine pepper & cheese, garlic (powder), salt, and seasoning (Italian). Mix cheese thoroughly and add in the seasoning. Place spoonful of mixture into the bottom of each space on tray.
4. After, top each space with pepperoni. Once ready, place into the oven for about eight to ten minutes. After this time, the cheese should be melted all the way through and light brown around the sides.
5. Lastly, remove, let cool, and serve with low-sugar sauce (marinara works best). Serve as a snack or side for a meat dish.

Chapter 4: Gourmet Recipe Ideas

Gourmet Idea #1: Tasty Chicken and Veggie Pot
Number of people served: 4 to 6
Time you'll need: 26 to 32 minutes

Calories: 238
Fats: 10.9g
Proteins: 27.6g
Carbs: 2.7g

What you'll require:

- Broccoli (one bag, frozen)
- Chicken (115g, shredded)
- Garlic Powder (as preferred)
- Soup (Cream of Mushroom, one can)
- Pepper (as preferred)
- Cheese (Cheddar 221g)

What you need to do:

1. First, prepare the oven to approximately 185 degrees Celsius.
2. Then, in a mixing container, toss in the various elements you will be using (chicken, cheese, and spices)
3. Next, add in soup.
4. Then, place the mixture into a baking container and insert it into the oven.
5. After, let cook in the oven for about twenty-five to thirty minutes.
6. Lastly, ensure that the soup has been thoroughly cooked and cheese properly melted. Serve with a side of crispy veggies or almond breadsticks.

Gourmet Idea #2: Delicious Low-sugar Chicken Meal

Number of people served: 4
Time you'll need: Approximately 30 minutes

Calories: 384

Fats: 21.1g
Proteins: 48.1g
Carbs: 3.2g

What you'll require:

- Cream (Sour, 221 g)
- Salt (9.5 g)
- Chicken (Breast, 1kg, no bone)
- Garlic (Powder, 14.5g)
- Pepper (4.5 g)
- Cheese (Parmesan, 165g, grated)

What you need to do:

1. First, prepare the oven to approximately 185 degrees Celsius.
2. Next, prepare a baking container with grease (or your choice such as spray)
3. After, in a mixing tray, add sour cream and a cup of cheese (Parmesan)
4. Then, place the chicken (breast) into the tray while spreading the mix atop each piece. Also, cover lightly with leftover cheese.
5. After that, insert the tray into the oven. Let it sit there for about twenty-seven to twenty-nine minutes.
6. Lastly, remove once thoroughly cooked and serve with your favorite low-carb side.

Gourmet Idea #3: Italian Chicken Dinner Delight
Number of people served: 2 to 4
Time you'll need: Approximately 25 minutes

Calories: 581
Fats: 41.1g
Proteins: 48.2g
Carbs: 6.1g

What you'll require:

- Garlic (Cloves, two, Minced)
- Tomatoes (Sun-dried, 65g)
- Spinach (221g, Chopped)
- Chicken (Breast, four)
- Paprika (8.5g)
- Cream (Heavy, 221 g)
- Garlic (Powder, 8.5g)
- Butter (14.5 g)
- Salt (8.5g)

What you need to do:

1. First, combine garlic (powder), paprika, and salt into mixing container. Upon completion, use this mixture to coat chicken lightly.
2. Next, fire up a skillet, or pan, and throw in two spoonfuls of butter at the base. Let the butter melt. After this, add in properly seasoned chicken and let cook thoroughly. This would take about five minutes per side. Please ensure chicken is cooked all the way through. Remove and place to one side.
3. Then, add in the rest of the elements: tomatoes, cream, and tomatoes. It will take about three minutes on low fire for the mix to thicken. After, toss in spinach and mix up everything for four more minutes.
4. Lastly, throw the chicken back into the mix so that all flavors can combine. Ensure that chicken is properly cooked and season further if needed. Serve with a side of veggies, zucchini pasta, or low-carb couscous.

Gourmet Idea #4: Yummy Lemon Beef Surprise
Number of people served: 4
Time you'll need: Approximately three hours

Calories: 507
Fats: 35.1g
Proteins: 44.8g
Carbs: 3.1g

What you'll require:

- Pepper (4.5g)
- Lemon (one)
- Garlic (Cloves, four, Crushed)
- Salt (4.5 g)
- Beef (one kg, Cubed)
- Parsley (26g, Minced)

What you need to do:

1. First, prepare the oven to approximately 167 degrees Celsius.
2. Then, prepare a baking container with foil lining.
3. Next, get a mixing container and cover beef (cubed) with juice (lemon), some zest (lemon), salt, and garlic as preferred. Once it is ready to taste, fold over foil to create a small package.
4. Then, when the package is ready, insert into the middle section of the oven and let sit for roughly three hours. This longer cooking time is intended to let the meat soften to its best point.
5. Lastly, remove the package and let sit for about five or six minutes. Cover meat with more juice (lemon) and sprinkle parsley on top. Serve with your favorite low-carb side.

Gourmet Idea #5: Gourmet Sirloin Option

Number of people served: 3 to 4
Time you'll need: 25 to 30 minutes

Calories: 389
Fats: 18.9g
Proteins: 47.1g
Carbs: 2.3g

What you'll require:

- Garlic (Cloves, four, Crushed)
- Oil (Olive, 12g)
- Pepper & salt (as preferred)
- Steak (Sirloin, 945g, Cubed)
- Butter (14.5 g)

What you need to do:

1. First, get an iron skillet or pan and place it on high heat and place oil (olive).
2. Next, add in pepper & salt to the steak as per your preference.
3. Once the steak has been seasoned according to your preference, place it in the hot skillet, or pan, with hot oil. Let the steak in the hot oil for about four minutes on each side. Turnover twice. Then remove. After, using the same skillet, or pan, toss in butter and garlic. Please ensure to move constantly, so the mix doesn't get burnt.

4. When the garlic is light or golden brown. Place meat for another couple of minutes on each side. Let simmer until the flavors are combined. Serve with your favorite side.

Gourmet Idea #6: Unbelievably Low-sugar Surprise
Number of people served: 4 to 6
Time you'll need: Approximately 20 minutes

Calories: 171
Fats: 11.8g
Proteins: 14.6g
Carbs: 2.9g

What you'll require:

- Cheese (Mozzarella, 100g, Shredded)
- Cheese (Parmesan, 75g, Grated)
- Cheddar Cheese (Shredded, 75g)
- Eggs (two)
- Ham (221g, Diced)

What you need to do:

1. First, set up oven to 185 degrees Celsius.
2. Next, get a mixing container so you can combine egg and the various types of cheeses (shredded). After thoroughly mixing, toss in ham (diced) and continue combining until mixture is evenly distributed.
3. After, get a baking container so it can be greased (your choice of grease).
4. Now, separate mixture into eight round balls or rolls.
5. Then, insert the baking container into the oven for approximately twenty minutes. The rolls will be ready once the cheese has melted, and a golden-brown crust has formed.
6. Lastly, remove the dish and allow it to cool. Serve with chicken or any other meat of your choice.

Gourmet Idea #7: Low-carb Salmon Delight

Number of people served: 3 to 4
Time you'll need: 18 to 24 minutes

Calories: 276
Fats: 19.1g
Proteins: 24.5g
Carbs: 3.7g

What you'll require:

- Rosemary (Fresh, two Springs)
- Lemon (55 g)
- Pepper (as preferred)
- Garlic (Cloves, three)
- Salt (4.5 g)

- Salmon (Filets, four)
- Butter (Unsalted, 8.5g)

What you need to do:

1. First, start out by setting the oven to 202 degrees Celsius.
2. Next, line baking container with a sheet of paper (parchment) and set to the side.
3. Then, rinse out filets (salmon) and pat down to try. Upon completion, place on the baking container with the skin facing down.
4. After, take some soft butter to cover the top of the filer. Also, add in some pepper & salt according to your liking.
5. Now, add the spices (rosemary) and the garlic. Cover the filet and insert it into the oven for roughly thirteen to sixteen minutes.
6. Lastly, remove the filet when thoroughly cooked. Add some juice (lemon) to add a tangy zest. Serve with a side of veggies for a nutritious meal.

Gourmet Idea #8: Shrimp-Avocado Treat
Number of people served: 4
Time you'll need: 30 to 35 minutes

Calories: 539
Fats: 45.2g
Proteins: 25.8g
Carbs: 6.1g

What you'll require:

- Onion (62.5g)
- Cooked shrimp (455g, Chopped)
- Eggs (two)
- Seasoning (Seafood, 4.5g)
- Juice (Lemon, 8.5g)
- Parsley (Fresh, 14.5g)
- Crab (Cooked 125g)
- Avocados (four)
- Cheese (Cheddar, 221 g, Shredded)

What you need to do:

1. First, start out by setting the oven to 177 degrees Celsius.
2. Then, in a mixing container, combine the ingredients: eggs, seasoning (seafood), juice (lemon), onion (chopped), cheese (cheddar), parsley, shrimp, and crab.
3. Next, as the stuffing is completed, cut up avocados in half and remove the pit. Then replace the pit with the stuffing.
4. Lastly, insert the avocados in the oven for roughly twenty-seven minutes. Remove from oven and serve with almond breadsticks.

Gourmet Idea #9: Gourmet Hot Pot Surprise
Number of people served: 4 to 6
Time you'll need: Approximately 45 minutes

Calories: 287
Fats: 20.8g
Proteins: 21.9g
Carbs: 4.8g

What you'll require:

- Cheese (Swiss, 70g, Shredded)
- Pepper (as preferred)
- Garlic (Cloves, four, Minced)
- Fish (Filet, your choice, 455g)
- Shrimp (455g)
- Cream (Heavy, 87g)
- Paprika (as preferred)
- Salt (as preferred)

What you need to do:

1. First, start out by setting the oven to 191 degrees Celsius.
2. Next, prepare a baking container with grease (your choice).
3. Then, cut the filet (fish) into small to medium-sized pieces and place them on the bottom of the baking container. Then, place a layer of shrimp on top of the fish. Add pepper & salt as per your liking.
4. After, when you have everything layered, add in garlic and heavy cream to cover. Upon liberally covering, add cheese (Swiss) on top. Add a touch of paprika for that tangy edge.
5. Now, insert into the oven for roughly sixteen to eighteen minutes. Check often to make sure it does not overcook.
6. Lastly, serve with almond bread!

Gourmet Idea #10: Low-carb Tuna Wraps Treat
Number of people served: 4
Time you'll need: About 10 minutes

Calories: 109
Fats: 5.7g
Proteins: 7.8g
Carbs: 7.1g

What you'll require:

- Yogurt (Greek, 50g)
- Wrap (Wheat, four)
- Bell Pepper (Red, 25g, Diced)
- Spinach (45g)
- Celery (65g, Diced)
- Tuna (one can)

What you need to do:

1. First, drain liquid from the can, and place tuna into a mixing container. Once this is in place, add in the red bell pepper, celery, and the Greek yogurt. Combine elements together well, so the vegetables and tuna are combined thoroughly.
2. Next, you are going to want to place the mixture into the middle of the whole-wheat wraps and top off with the spinach.
3. Serve with veggie chips and lemonade for a refreshing brunch treat.

Chapter 5: Quick and Easy Recipe Ideas

Quick and Easy Idea #1: Quick and Easy Veggie Treat

Number of people served: 4
Time you'll need: 35 to 40 minutes

Calories: 51

Fats: 3.1 g
Proteins: 4.5 g
Carbs: 2.3 g

What you'll require:

- Egg (whites, two)
- Spinach (221g, chopped)
- Eggs (whole, two)
- Pepper (Bell, one)
- Salsa (14.5g)
- Onion (35g, chopped)
- Pepper & salt (as preferred)

What you need to do:

1. First, place the pan over medium fire. Once it is warm, throw in some oil (olive) and start by placing spinach and onion until reaching consistency to your preference. Season with pepper plus salt. Add more salsa if you wish.

2. Next, let your vegetables cook, cut up a bell pepper in two slices to create a small bowl. Upon completion, add the spinach mix to the pepper bowls and the open an egg on top.

3. Then, insert into the oven for about 25 to 28 minutes. Make sure to see that egg is thoroughly prepared.

4. Lastly, serve as a side to your favorite meat dish.

Quick and Easy Idea #2: Spicy Egg and Veggie Dash
Number of people served: 12
Time you'll need: 30 to 35 minutes

Calories: 242

Fats: 21.7 g
Proteins: 10.2 g
Carbs: 1.1 g

What you'll require:

- Bacon (in strips, 11)

- Onion (Powder, 4.5g)
- Garlic (Powder, 4.5g)
- Cheese (cream, 95g)
- Pepper & salt (as preferred)
- Eggs (8)
- Peppers (Jalapeno, four, Chopped)
- Cheese (Cheddar, 121 g)

What you need to do:

1. First, fire up the oven to 165 degrees Celsius.
2. Then, fire up bacon until crispy.
3. Next, in another container, mix up chopped jalapenos, eggs, cheese (cream), and seasoning. Toss in leftover bacon grease.
4. Then, take a muffin baking container and fill the edge of each space with bacon. Upon completion, pour in the mix down the middle of each space. Fill up to about 2/3 of the way. This is important as eggs will rise.
5. After, add some cheese (cheddar) and some jalapeno to provide spice. Insert into the oven and let cook for about 22 to 24 minutes. These will be ready when eggs are thoroughly done and fluffy.
6. Lastly, remove and serve as a snack or an appetizer.

Quick and Easy Idea #3: Low-sugar Hot Cake Surprise

Number of people served: 10
Time you'll need: Approximately 20 minutes

Calories: 133
Fats: 11.8 g
Proteins: 5.3 g
Carbs: 1.9 g

What you'll require:

- Flour (Almond, 221 g)
- Eggs (4)
- Milk (Almond, Non-sugar, 36.5g)
- Extract (Vanilla, 7.5g)
- Baking Powder (4.7g)
- Oil (Olive, 18.5g)

What you need to do:

1. First, in a mixing container, mix up baking powder, extract (vanilla), milk (almond), flour (almond), and eggs. Please ensure all clumps are removed.
2. Next, use a tablespoon to place mixture into pan or skillet. Prepare these as you would regular pancakes.
3. Last, top with butter or non-sugar syrup.

Quick and Easy Idea #4: Cheesy Veggie Bites

Number of people served: 4
Time you'll need: Approximately 30 minutes

Calories: 161
Fats: 11.6 g
Proteins: 11.4 g
Carbs: 5.1 g

What you'll require:

- Flour (Almond, 36.5g)
- Onion (36.5g, minced)
- Seasoning (Mexican, 8.5g)
- Mozzarella (221g, shredded)
- Broccoli (225g)
- Salt (as preferred)
- Garlic (clove, one, minced)
- Cilantro (17.5g)

- Egg (one)
- Pepper (as preferred)

What you need to do:

1. First, set up 201 degrees Celsius.
2. Next, prepare a baking container by lining with parchment paper.
3. Then, steam broccoli in a pot (5 minutes) or microwave (1-2 minutes). Tenderize broccoli to make chopping easier.
4. After, cut up broccoli into small chunks. Throw everything into mixing container (parsley, cheese, flour, egg, and spices). Mix up thoroughly until evenly distributed.
5. Now, roll up into a small ball and distribute evenly throughout the baking container.
6. Once completed, cover with some oil (olive) and insert it into the oven for about 26 to 28 minutes.
7. Lastly, serve with low-carb dip as a snack.

Quick and Easy Idea #5: Low-carb Pudding Dee-light
Number of people served: 4
Time you'll need: 18 to 20 minutes

Calories: 132
Fats: 12.1g
Proteins: 13.8g
Carbs: 1.4g

What you'll require:
- Coconut (125g, shredded)
- Almonds (221g, chopped)
- Chia seed (221g)
- Milk (almond, 225g)

What you need to do:
1. First, measure out all of the fixings and add to the Instant Pot, stirring well.
2. Then, secure the lid and select the high setting (2-5 minutes)
3. Lastly, quick release the pressure and place the pudding into four serving glasses.

Quick and Easy Idea #6: Tangy Egg Salad

Number of people served: 4 to 5
Time you'll need: 26 to 32 minutes

Calories: 314
Fats: 25.7g
Proteins: 15.4g
Carbs: 1.4g

What you'll require:
- Bacon (strips, five, raw)
- Paprika (smoked, 14.5)
- Eggs (large, 10)
- Onion (green, 36.5g)

- Mayonnaise (125g)
- Mustard (Dijon, 45g)
- Pepper & salt (as preferred)

Also required: 6-7-inch baking container

What you need to do:
1. First, grease up all sides of the pan inside of pot on the trivet. Toss one cup of cold water in the bottom of the Instant Pot and add the steam rack.
2. Next, open up eggs in a pan.
3. Then, insert pan on rack. Secure the lid and set the timer for 6 minutes (high-pressure). Natural release the pressure to remove pan.
4. After, remove any moisture. Flip pan over on a wooden cutting board for egg loaf to release. Cut up and place it into a mixing dish.
5. Now, clean the Instant Pot container and choose the sauté function (medium fire). Prepare bacon till crispy.
6. After that, add in chopped eggs with mustard, mayo, paprika, pepper, and salt. Top with green onion.
7. Lastly, serve as a side with your favorite meat dish.

Quick and Easy Idea #7: Cheesy Egg Cups
Number of people served: 4
Time you'll need: 12 to 16 minutes

Calories: 117
Fats: 8.8g
Proteins: 8.7g
Carbs: 1.8g

What you'll require:

- Eggs (four)
- Cheese (Cheddar, 125g, shredded)
- Veggies (diced, your choice, veggies tomatoes, mushrooms, and/or peppers, 221g)
- Milk (low-fat, non-sugar, 221g)
- Pepper & salt (as preferred)
- Cilantro (chopped, 125g)

What you'll require for the Topping:
- Cheese (shredded, your choice, 221g)

Also Required:
1. Jars (medium, four)
2. Water (0.5L)

What you need to do:
1. First, whisk up cheese, veggies, pepper, eggs, milk (low-fat), salt, and cilantro.
1. Next, combine the mix into each jar. Tighten lids (not too tight) to keep water from entering the egg mix.
2. Then, arrange the trivet in the Instant Pot and add the water. Arrange the jars on the trivet and set the timer for 5 minutes (high pressure). When done, quick release the pressure, and top with the rest of the cheese (½ cup).
3. Lastly, broil if you like for 2 to 4 minutes till the cheese is browned to your preference.

Quick and Easy Idea #8: Asparagus Appetizer/Side Salad
Number of people served: 4 to 6
Time you'll need: 18 to 22 minutes

Calories: 221
Fats: 8.6g
Proteins: 15.7g
Carbs: 8.1g

What you'll require:

- Red potatoes (small, 455g)
- Asparagus (fresh, trimmed and chopped lengthwise)
- Tuna (2 tins)
- Olives (Greek, 125g, pit removed)
- Dressing (Italian, low sugar, 45g)

What you need to do:

1. First, chop potatoes and let soak in water for about 5 minutes to let starch drain.
2. Next, put water in the pot, about 2 inches, and heat up to a boiling point. Throw in chopped potatoes to cook for about 12 to 14 minutes.
3. Then, in the remaining 2 to 4 minutes of cooking potatoes, add asparagus to the water.
4. After, turn off the heat, remove water from asparagus and potatoes and then place it into ice water.
5. Lastly, serve with tuna and olives as an appetizer or side for a chicken or fish dish.

Quick and Easy Idea #9: Low-carb Pork Treat
Number of people served: 4 to 6
Time you'll need: 18 to 22 minutes

Calories: 221
Fats: 8.6g
Proteins: 15.7g
Carbs: 8.1g

What you'll require:

- Pork (tenderloin, 455g)
- Salt (14.5g)
- Pepper (18.5g)
- Oil (Olive, 75g)
- Cider (apple, 95g)
- Syrup (maple, non-sugar, 25g)
- Vinegar (apple cider)

What you need to do:

1. First, set up your oven to 190 degrees Celsius.
2. Next, cut up tenderloin into two pieces or to fit in the pan or skillet you are using. Transfer into another container.
3. Then, put oil in pan, or skillet, and then fire up for about 6 to 8 minutes. Toss in vinegar, syrup, and cider while adding pepper until boiling point. Make sure to remove bits stuck to the bottom.
4. After, throw in meat. Prepare thoroughly until the mixture is reduced to glazed texture.
5. Lastly, remove and serve while adding sauce for glazing. Serve with a side of veggies.

Quick and Easy Idea #10: Easy Fish Delight
Number of people served: 4 to 6   Time you'll need: 18 to 22 minutes

Calories: 257
Fats: 8.8g
Proteins: 25.7g
Carbs: 9.2g

What you'll require:

- Breadcrumbs (low-carb, 56g)
- Oil (Olive, 45g)
- Dill (fresh, 45g, snipped)
- Salt (10.5g)
- Pepper (5g)
- Filet (tilapia or salmon, 50g per filet)
- Juice (lemon, 25g)
- Lemon (wedges)

What you need to do:

1. First, set up the oven to 186 degrees Celsius. Add the pepper, oil (olive), dill (fresh), salt, and juice (lemon).
2. Next, add filet (fish of your choice) into a baking container which has been previously coated with grease. Add breadcrumbs on top of fish patting down to so they stick. Coat both sides.
3. Then, let sit in the oven until fish is tender, roughly for 12 to 14 minutes.
4. Lastly, serve with veggies and add lemon wedges on top.

Chapter 6: Low-Carb Recipe Ideas

Low-Carb Recipe Idea #1: Balsamic Roast Delight
Number of people served: 4 to 6
Time you'll need: 35 to 40 minutes

Calories: 51
Fats: 3.1 g
Proteins: 4.5 g
Carbs: 2.3 g

What you'll require:
- Chuck roast (one, no bone, 1.5kg)
- Onion (chopped, 55g)
- Water (0.5L)
- Ground pepper (black, 14.5g)
- Garlic (powder, 14.5g)
- Salt (kosher, 14.5g)
- Vinegar (balsamic, 14.5g)
- Xanthan gum (25g)

For Garnishing:
- Fresh parsley (chopped, 20g)

What you need to do:
1. First, combine the garlic powder, salt, and pepper and spread on the meat to prepare the seasoning.
2. Next, utilize the skillet to sear the meat. Add in the vinegar and deglaze the skillet, or pan, while you let cook for another couple of minutes.
3. Then, toss in onion into a pot along with (two cups) boiling water into the mixture. Cover with a top and allow simmer for thirty to forty minutes on medium-low heat.
4. After, remove meat from pot and add to a cutting surface. Shred up into chunks and throw away any fat and/or bones.
5. Now, add in the xanthan gum to the broth and mix up briskly. Place the thoroughly cooked meat back into the pan to heat up.
6. Lastly, serve with a favorite side dish.

Low-Carb Recipe Idea #2: Burger Calzone Treat

Number of people served: 6
Time you'll need: 25 to 30 minutes

Calories: 400
Fats: 25.1g
Proteins: 24.5 g
Carbs: 2.6 g

What you'll require:

- Mayonnaise (45g)
- Onion (yellow, one diced)
- Beef (ground, 750g, lean)
- Cheese (cheddar, 75g, shredded)
- Flour (Almond, 95g)
- Cheese (Mozzarella, 75g, shredded)
- Egg (one)
- Bacon (4 thin strips)
- Dill pickle (4 spears)

- Cheese (cream, 95g)

What you need to do:
1. First, program the oven to 185 degrees Celsius. Set up a baking container with parchment paper.
2. Next, chop up pickles into lengthy spears. Set to one side when completed.
3. Then, to prepare the crust, combine half of the cream cheese and the mozzarella. Insert into microwave 30 seconds. Upon melting, add egg and almond flour to prepare the dough. Set aside.
4. After, set the beef to fire on the stove using a medium temp setting.
5. Now, cook bacon (microwave for approximately four minutes or on the stovetop with pan or skillet). Upon cooling, break up into bits.
6. Now, dice up an onion and toss into the beef to cook until tenderized. Throw in bacon, pickle bits, cheddar cheese, the rest of the cream cheese, and mayonnaise. Move briskly.
7. After that, roll the dough into a prepared baking container. Place the mixture into the middle of the container. Fold up ends and side to create the calzone.
8. Lastly, insert into until brown or about 12 to 14 minutes. Let it rest for 10 minutes before cutting up.

Low-Carb Recipe Idea #3: Steak Skillet Nacho

Number of people served: 3 to 4
Time you'll need: 26 to 33 minutes
Calories: 376
Fats: 31.5g
Proteins: 19.4g
Carbs: 6.1 g

What you'll require:

- Cheese (Cheddar, 75g)
- Coconut oil (45g)
- Butter (15g)
- Beef (Steak, round tip, 1kg)
- Cauliflower (750g)

- Turmeric (15g)
- Chili (powder, 15g)
- Cheese (Monterey Jack, 75g)

For Garnishing:

- Sour cream (25g)
- Jalapeno (canned, 20g, slices)
- Avocado (105g)

What you need to do:

1. First, set up oven temp to 176 degrees Celsius.
2. Next, prepare the cauliflower into chip-like shapes.
3. After, combine the chili powder, turmeric, and coconut oil in a mixing container.
4. Then, throw in cauliflower and add it to a container. Set the timer for 18 to 24 minutes.
5. Now, over a med-high fire in a cast iron pan, place butter. Fire up until both sides are thoroughly done, flipping only one time. Let it sit for six to nine minutes. Slice up thinly and add in some pepper and salt to the meat.
6. After that, move the florets to the pan and add in the steak bits. Top it off with the cheese and bake six to nine more minutes.
7. Lastly, serve with your favorite side of veggies.

Low-Carb Recipe Idea #4: Portobello Burger Meal

Number of people served: 4
Time you'll need: 22 to 27 minutes

Calories: 327
Fats: 23.1g
Proteins:19.4g
Carbs: 6.1 g

What you'll require:
- Mushroom (Portobello, 6 caps)
- Beef (ground, 455g, lean)
- Pepper (Black, 6g, ground)
- Worcestershire sauce (14.5g)
- Salt (pink or kosher, 12g)

- Cheese (cheddar, 56g or 6 slices)
- Oil (avocado, 12g)

What you need to do:
1. First, remove the stem, rinse, and dab dry the mushrooms.
2. Then, combine the salt, pepper, beef, and Worcestershire sauce in a mixing container. Shape into patties.
3. After, fire up the oil (medium fire). Let caps simmer about four to five minutes on each side.
4. Next, move the mushrooms to a bowl, utilizing the same pan, prepare the patties for six minutes, turn, and prepare another six minutes until ready.
5. Now, combine the cheese to the patties and cover for about a minute to melt the cheese.
6. Lastly, add a mushroom cap to burgers along with the desired garnish to serve.

Low-Carb Recipe Idea #5: Low-carb Super Chili
Number of people served: 4
Time you'll need: 20 to 24 minutes

Calories: 319
Fats: 24.1g
Proteins:39.2g
Carbs: 3.4g

What you'll require for the Chili:

- Stock (beef or chicken, 25g)
- Steak (1kg, cubed into 1-inch cubes)
- Leeks (sliced, 25g)
- Cumin (4g)
- Cayenne pepper (ground, 4g)
- Pepper (black, 4g)
- Salt (4g)
- Whole tomatoes (canned with juices, 221g)
- Chili powder (2.5g)

Additional Toppings:

- Cheese (cheddar, 221g, shredded)
- Sour cream (95g)
- Cilantro (fresh, 25g, chopped)
- Avocado (one half, sliced or cubed)

What you need to do:

1. First, toss all of the fixings into the cooker - except the toppings.
2. Then, use the cooker's high setting for about six hours.
3. Lastly, serve and add the toppings.

Low-Carb Recipe Idea #6: "You won't believe it's low-carb" Chicken Parmesan
Number of people served: 2 to 4
Time you'll need: 34 to 40 minutes

Calories: 586
Fats: 31.4g
Proteins:55.5g
Carbs: 2.7g

What you'll require:
- Rinds (pork, 221g)
- Sauce (Marinara, 45g)
- Chicken (breast, 455g)
- Cheese (parmesan, 56g)
- Garlic (powder, 12g)
- Pepper & salt (as preferred)
- Egg (one)
- Cheese (Mozzarella, 125g, shredded)
- Oregano (12g)

What you need to do:
1. First, set up an oven temp setting of 165 degrees Celsius.
2. Next, utilize a food processor to mash rinds and cheese (parmesan). Add them to a mixing container.
3. After, pound chicken breasts until they are about one-half inch thick. Whisk up egg and dip chicken in for the egg wash. Place the chicken into crumbs.
4. Then, distribute the breasts on a lightly greased baking container evenly. Add in seasonings and insert them into the oven for approximately 23 to 26 minutes.
5. Now, cover with the marinara sauce over each serving. Top with the mozzarella and bake for 12 to 14 minutes.
6. Lastly, serve with a bed of spinach.

Low-Carb Recipe Idea #7: Tangy Coconut Chicken

Number of people served: 4 to 5
Time you'll need: 25 to 28 minutes

Calories: 492
Fats: 39.7g
Proteins:28.9g
Carbs: 2.3g

What you'll require for the Tenders:

- Egg (large, one)

- Onion (powder, 8.5g)
- Curry (powder, 18.5g)
- Pork rinds (Crumbled, 125g)
- Chicken (thighs, 1kg, no bone or skin, about 6 to 8 pieces)
- Coriander (14.5g)
- Coconut (shredded, 95g, unsweetened)
- Garlic (powder, 8.5g)
- Pepper & salt (as preferred)

What you'll require for spicy and sweet mango sauce dip:

- Sour cream (25g)
- Ginger (ground, 14.5g)
- Mango extract (15g)
- Mayonnaise (25g)
- Sugar-free ketchup(25g)
- Cayenne pepper (14g)
- Liquid stevia (7 to 8 drops)
- Garlic (powder, 8.5g)
- Red pepper (flakes, 5g)

What you need to do:
1. First, program oven to 185 degrees Celsius.
2. Then, whisk the eggs and debone the thighs. Slice them into strips (skins on).
3. Next, add the spices, coconut, and pork rinds to a zipper-type bag. Add the chicken, shake, and place on a wire rack. Bake for about 14 minutes. Flip them over and continue baking for another 18 minutes.
4. Lastly, combine the sauce components and stir well. Serve with your favorite side of veggies or salad.

Low-Carb Recipe Idea #8: Slow cook Chicken Casserole
Number of people served: 3 to 4
Time you'll need: 35 to 45 minutes
Calories: 224
Fats: 9.4g
Proteins:30.4g
Carbs: 5.7g

What you'll require:

- Chicken breasts (two in cubes)
- Bay leaf (one)
- Cheese (Mozzarella, 221g, shredded)
- Tomato sauce (256g or one tine)
- Seasoning (Italian, 14.5g)
- Salt (5.5g)
- Pepper (4g)
- Optional: slow cooker (2-quart)

What you need to do:

1. First, remove the bones from the chicken and chop it into cubes. Add them to the slow cooker.
2. Next, pour in the sauce over the chicken and add the spices. Stir and cook on the low setting for thirty to forty minutes.
3. Lastly, serve with the cheese as a topping.

Low-Carb Recipe Idea #9: Low-carb Roll Up Treat
Number of people served: 2 to 4
Time you'll need: 15 to 20 minutes

Calories: 191
Fats: 7.9g
Proteins:15.6g
Carbs: 1.9g

What you'll require:

- Eggs (large, 6)
- Milk (221g)
- Garlic (powder, 14.5g)
- Salt (kosher, 9.5g)
- Pepper (Black, 9.5g, freshly ground)
- Butter (11g)
- Chives (chopped, 5g)
- Bacon (slices, 12)
- Cheese (cheddar, 105g)

What you need to do:

- First, in mixing container, whisk up eggs together along with milk and garlic (powder). Add in salt & pepper as preferred.
- Next, in skillet or pan, melt butter over medium fire. Toss in eggs and scramble for 2 to 4 minutes. Toss in chives.
- Then, on a cutting surface, cut up bacon slices. Place cheddar on the bottom and then toss in a bunch of eggs. Roll up very closely.
- Lastly, place rolls back into pan, or skillet with the seam facing down. Remove once crispy. Serve with whole-grain toast.

Low-Carb Recipe Idea #10: Cauliflower Cheese Surprise
Number of people served: 2 to 4
Time you'll need: 10 to 20 minutes

Calories: 164
Fats: 6.5g
Proteins: 16.3g
Carbs: 2.4g

What you'll require:

- Cauliflower (one Head, about 256g)
- Eggs (two)
- Cheese (parmesan, 75g)
- Oregano (35g)
- Cheese (cheddar, 75g, shredded)

What you need to do:

- First, cut up cauliflower into individual florets. Place them into a food processor until the texture appears similar to rice. You could also grate if you don't have a processor.
- Then, in a mixing container, combine cauliflower, eggs, cheese (parmesan), and the oregano. Mix up until even and add salt & pepper.
- After, fire up a skillet, or pan, over medium fire. Todd mixture into the pan. Pat down to form a patty. Exert pressure using a spatula. Cook for 4 to 6 minutes. Turn over and repeat on the other side.
- Lastly, sprinkle cheese until it is melted. Make "sandwiches" by putting two pieces together. Serve as a snack or side to your favorite meat dish.

Chapter 7: 7-day Sample Low Sugar Diet Plan

In this chapter, we are presenting a 7-day sample plan to give you an idea of how you can put together a winning combination of healthy foods. Please bear in mind that this is only a guide. So, feel free to customize this plan as you get more experience and develop your own style.

Week One			
Day / Meal	**Breakfast**	**Lunch**	**Dinner**
Monday	Fresh fruit bowl topped with granola and honey	Veggie and chicken club sandwich on whole wheat bread	Chicken and veggie casserole
Tuesday	Spicy breakfast burritos	Bean soup with croutons	Grilled salmon and veggies
Wednesday	Scrambled eggs, bacon and a slice of whole-grain toast	Mixed garden salad, fresh veggies, and grilled chicken	Sirloin and veggies surprise
Thursday	Low-sugar cereal with low-fat dairy milk	Steak and potatoes with a side of crispy veggies	Chicken fajitas with mashed potatoes
Friday	Veggie cheesy bits	Grilled salmon, sautéed veggies with garlic whole wheat toast	Roast beef club sandwich with crispy plantain bits
Saturday	Low-sugar whole grain flapjacks	Spicy chicken fajita burritos	Veggie pizza with small salad
Sunday	Whole grain veggie breakfast wraps	Tangy Mexican bean bowl with guacamole	Chicken noodles and sautéed veggies

PART IV

Chapter 1: Introduction to the Heart-Healthy Diet

A heart-healthy diet is incredibly important. The truth is, you must be able to manage your diet well if you want to be healthy. The average diet is actually incredibly unhealthy for the heart, and the sooner that you are able to change up how you treat yourself and your body, the better off you will be. The average person consumes far too much salt and not enough of the important fruits and veggies that they need. As a result, they wind up with problems with their blood sugars, their blood pressure, and cholesterol levels. It is important to understand that your heart is one of the most important parts of your body—you cannot live without it. You need to keep it healthy. If you want to ensure that you can keep yourself healthy, you need to make sure that you eat the foods that will help you to nourish it readily. The sooner that you can do so, the better off you will be. This book is here to provide you with plenty of heart-healthy meals that you can enjoy that will help you to stay as healthy as possible.

The Rules of the Heart-Healthy Diet

Before we begin, let's go over some of the most important rules that go into the heart-healthy diet. These are rules that will help you to ensure that your body is kept as healthy as possible with foods that will nourish you well. Now, on this diet, you can expect to follow these rules:

1. **Decrease saturated and trans fats:** These are fats that are no good for anyone. Instead, it is recommended that you focus entirely on monounsaturated and polyunsaturated fats. These come from primarily vegetarian options—common sources include olive and canola oils, avocado, nuts, and fatty fish.

2. **Increase fruits and veggies:** Your body needs the vitamins and minerals in fruits and veggies to stay as healthy as possible. You should be consuming at least seven to nine servings per day to keep your body healthy and on track.

3. **Consume more fiber:** Typically, on this diet, you want to up your fiber intake. Fiber is necessary to keep your body regular. It also helps with the way that you will naturally digest and absorb nutrients. You need both soluble and insoluble sources to stay as healthy as possible. Soluble fiber will aid in regulating your body and is fantastic for the heart. Insoluble fiber is there to help you regulate your weight and pass waste.

4. **Make the switch to plant proteins whenever possible:** You will also see that this diet advocates for more vegetarian options and less meat. While you can still eat meat, it is highly recommended that you choose to put in at least three servings of vegetable proteins, and you limit red meats down to just once a week. Twice a week, you should eat skinless poultry, and twice a week, you should enjoy fish.

5. **Up your whole grain intake:** This is essential to ensuring that you are not just consuming a bunch of empty carbs that aren't doing anything for you. By shifting to whole grains, you get more of the fiber that you need, and they are also usually full of better nutritional content as well.

6. **Limiting sweets:** If you are going to enjoy sweets, it is usually recommended that you cut out sugar or sugar-sweetened dishes. While you do not have to completely eliminate them, you should, at the very least, monitor and regulate intake.

7. **Low-fat dairy products:** You should have between two and three servings of dairy per day, but they ought to be reduced fat.

8. **Drink in moderation:** Alcohol is okay—but is not really encouraged either. If you must drink alcohol, make sure that you do so in moderation, which is typically defined as no more than one per day for women and no more than two per day for men.

The Benefits of the Heart-Healthy Diet

The heart-healthy diet has all sorts of benefits that are worth enjoying, and you should be able to treat these as motivation. If you find that you are struggling to enjoy this diet, consider these benefits to give you that added boost. Ultimately, the heart is the key to the body, and if you can keep it healthier, you will enjoy a better life for reasons such as:

- **Preventing heart disease:** When you limit salts, sweets, red meats, and everything else, you will help your heart remain healthier, and in doing so, you will reduce your risk of both stroke and heart disease.

- **Keeping your body healthier:** This diet is often recommended to older people, and this is for good reason—it keeps the body more agile by reducing the risk of frailty and muscle weakness.

- **Cutting the risk of Alzheimer's disease:** This diet helps your cholesterol, blood sugar, and blood vessel health, all of which are believed to aid in reducing the risk of both dementia and Alzheimer's disease.

- **Cutting the risk of Parkinson's disease:** Similarly, because this diet will be high in antioxidants, it has been found to cut the risk of Parkinson's disease significantly.

- **Longer lifespan:** This diet, because it lowers your risk of heart disease and cancer, is actually able to reduce your risk of death by around 20%.

- **Healthier mind:** If you suffer from anxiety or depression, this diet can actually help to alleviate some of the symptoms, or keep them at bay in the future. Between the healthy fats, rich vegetable content, and the boost to your gut bacteria, you will find that your body and mind both are healthier than ever.

- **It helps manage weight:** If you have struggled with your weight for some time, you may find that using this diet will actually help you to manage it, thanks to the fact that you'll be cutting out much of the foods that tend to lead to weight gain in the first place. You'll be able to enjoy a healthier body as the weight fades away through enjoying this diet.

Chapter 2: Heart-Healthy Savory Meals

Shrimp Scampi and Zoodles

Ingredients

- Butter (1 Tbsp., unsalted)
- Dry white wine (0.5 c.)
- Garlic (4 cloves, grated)
- Lemon juice (2 Tbsp.)
- Lemon zest (1 Tbsp.)
- Linguini (6 oz.)
- Olive oil (2 Tbsp.)
- Parsley (0.25 c., chopped)
- Red pepper flakes (0.25 tsp.)
- Shrimp (1.5 lbs., peeled and deveined—preferably large)
- Zucchini (3, spiralized)

Instructions

1. Start by preparing the pasta based on the instructions on the package. Keep 0.25 c. of the water to the side and drain the rest. Put pasta back in the pot.
2. Combine the shrimp, garlic, oil, salt, and pepper to taste and allow it to sit for five minutes.
3. Prepare a skillet and cook your shrimp in the garlicky oil over medium and garlic until done, roughly 3-4 minutes per side with a large count. Move shrimp to plate without the oil.
4. Add zest and pepper to the oil, along with the wine. Scrape the brown bits and reduce to 50%. Mix in lemon juice and butter, then toss the zoodles in.
5. After 2 minutes, add in shrimp, pasta, and combine well. Mix in water if necessary and toss with parsley.

Ingredients

- Baby kale (5 oz.)
- Chicken thighs (2 lbs.)
- Dijon mustard (1 tsp)
- Lemon juice (2 Tbsp.)
- Olive oil (2 Tbsp.)
- Orange (1, cut into 6 pieces)
- Salt and pepper
- Stale bread (8 oz., torn up into bite-sized bits)

Instructions

1. Warm oven to 425F. As it preheats, warm up half of your oil into a skillet. Then, salt and pepper the chicken, cooking it skin-side down in the oil. After 6 or 7 minutes, when the skin is golden, remove it to a

baking sheet. Then, toss in the orange wedges and roast another 10 minutes until the chicken is completely cooked.

2. Reserve 2 Tbsp. of the chicken fat in the pot and then return it to low heat. Toss in the bread chunks, coating them in the fat. Add a quick sprinkle of salt and pepper, then cook until toasted, usually about 8 minutes or so. Set aside.

3. Warm pan on medium-low, then toss in lemon juice. Deglaze the pan for a minute, then remove from heat. Combine with Dijon mustard and juice from roasted oranges. Mix in remaining oil.

4. Add kale and croutons to skillet to mix well, coating it in the mixture. Serve immediately with chicken.

Shrimp Taco Salad

Ingredients

- 3 Fresh lime juice (3 tbsp.)
- Avocado (1)
- Cayenne pepper sauce (1 tsp.)
- Cilantro leaves (1 c.)
- Corn chips (such as Fritos-- 2 c.)
- Extra-virgin olive oil (0.25 c.)
- Fresh corn (3 pieces)
- Ground coriander (0.25 tsp.)
- Ground cumin (0.25 tsp.)
- Salt
- Shrimp (1 lb.)
- Watermelon (2 c.)
- Zucchini (2 medium)

Instructions

1. Set up your grill to medium heat.
2. First grill the corn until it begins to char, usually about 10 minutes, with the occasional turn. At the same time, allow zucchini to grill for around 6 minutes until beginning to soften. Shrimp requires 2-4 minutes until cooked through, flipping once.
3. Combine your oil, juice, and seasonings, with just a pinch of salt.
4. Remove the kernels off of your corn and slice up your zucchini. Place zucchini and avocado onto a plate, topping it with the corn, then the watermelon, and finally the shrimp. You can leave it as is until you're ready to eat—it keeps for about a day in the fridge.
5. To serve, top with the chips (crumbled) and the dressing mix.

Chicken, Green Bean, Bacon Pasta

Ingredients

- Bacon (4 slices)
- Chicken breast (1 lb., cut into bite-sized bits)
- Egg yolk (1 large)
- Green beans (fresh—8 oz., trimmed and cut in half)
- Half-and-half (2 Tbsp.)
- Lemon juice (2 Tbsp.)
- Parmesan cheese (1 oz., grated—about 0.5 c.)
- Penne pasta (12 oz.)
- Scallions (2, sliced thinly)
- Spinach (5 oz.)

Instructions

1. Prepare pasta according to the package. Then, at the last minute of cooking, toss in the beans. Drain, reserving 0.5 c. of the cooking water. Leave pasta mix in the pot.
2. In a skillet, start preparing the bacon until crisp. Dry on a paper towel and then break into bits when cooled. Clean pan, reserving 1 Tbsp. of bacon fat.
3. On medium heat, cook the chicken until browning and cooked all the way. Then, off of the burner, toss in the lemon juice.
4. Mix together your egg and half-and-half in a separate container. Then, dump it to coat in the pasta and green beans, then toss in the chicken, spinach, and cheese. Mix well to coat. Add pasta water if needed, 0.25 c. at a time. Mix in the scallions, then top with bacon. Serve.

Heart-Healthy "Fried" Chicken

Ingredients

- Blackening seasoning (2 tsp.)
- Buttermilk (0.5 c.)
- Chicken drumsticks (2 lb., skinless)
- Cornflakes (4 c.)
- Olive oil (1 Tbsp.)
- Parsley (0.5 c., chopped)
- Salt (a pinch to taste)

Instructions

1. Get ready to bake the chicken at a temperature of 375F and make sure that you've got something to bake on that is currently protected.
2. Mix buttermilk, seasoning, and a touch of salt.
3. Crush cornflakes and put them in a second bowl. Combine with the oil and parsley.
4. Prep chicken by dipping first in buttermilk, letting it drip, then coating in cornflakes. Bake for 30-35 minutes.

Turkey Burgers and Slaw

Ingredients

Slaw

- Apple (1, matchstick-cut)
- Cabbage (8 oz., thinly sliced)
- Honey (1 Tbsp.)
- Jalapeno (1, thinly sliced and seeded)
- Lime juice (3 Tbsp.)
- Red wine vinegar (1 Tbsp.)
- Salt and pepper, to your preference

Burgers

- Buns (4, toasted lightly)
- Chili paste (1.5 Tbsp.)
- Ginger (1 Tbsp., grated)
- Olive oil (2 Tbsp.)
- Onion (0.5 chopped)
- Soy sauce (1 Tbsp.)
- Turkey (1 lb., ground up)

Instructions

1. Mix together the liquids for the slaw and the seasoning. Mix well, then toss in the slaw ingredients. Set aside.
2. Prepare your burger mixture, adding everything together, but the oil and the buns somewhere that you can mix them up. Combine well, then form four patties.
3. Prepare to your preference. Grills work well, or you choose to, you could use a cast iron pan with the oil. Cook until done.
4. Serve on buns with slaw and any other condiments you may want.

Slow Cooked Shrimp and Pasta
Ingredients

- Acini di pepe (4 oz., cooked to package specifications)
- Basil (0.25 c., chopped fresh)
- Diced tomatoes (14.5 oz. can)
- Feta (2 oz., crumbled)
- Garlic (2 cloves, minced)
- Kalamata olives (8, chopped)
- Olive oil (1 Tbsp.)
- Pinch of salt
- Rosemary (1.5 tsp fresh, chopped)
- Shrimp (8 oz., fresh or frozen)
- Sweet red bell pepper (1, chopped)
- White wine (0.5 c.) or chicken broth (o.5 c.)
- Zucchini (1 c., sliced)

Instructions

1. Thaw, peel, and devein shrimp. Set aside in fridge until ready to use them.
2. Coat your slow cooker insert with cooking spray, then add in tomato, zucchini tomatoes, bell pepper, and garlic.
3. Cook on low for 4 hours, or high for 2 hours. Mix in shrimp. Then, keep heat on high. Cook covered for 30 minutes.
4. Prepare pasta according to the instructions on the packaging.
5. Mix in the olives, rosemary, basil, oil, and salt.
6. Serve with pasta topped with shrimp, then topped with feta.

Chapter 3: Heart-Healthy Sweet Treats

Chocolate Mousse

Ingredients

- Avocado (1 large, pitted and skinned)
- Cocoa powder (2 Tbsp., unsweetened)
- Nondairy milk of choice (3 Tbsp., unsweetened)
- Nonfat vanilla Greek yogurt (0.25 c.)
- Semi-sweet baking chocolate (2 oz., melted and cooling)
- Sweetener packet if desired.
- Vanilla extract (1 tsp.)

Instructions

1. Prepare by putting all ingredients but sugar into a food processor. Combine well. Taste. If you want it sweeter, add in some sweetener as well.
2. Chill in your fridge until you are ready to serve.

Baked Pears
Ingredients

- Almonds (0.25 c., chopped)
- Brown sugar (0.33 c., can sub with honey)
- Butter (2 oz., melted, or coconut oil if you prefer vegan)
- Ground cinnamon (1 tsp)
- Ripe pears (3)
- Rolled oats (0.5 c.)
- Salt (a pinch)
- Sugar (pinch)

Instructions

1. Set oven to 400 F.
2. Incorporate all dry ingredients. Then, mix half of your melted butter.
3. Cut your pears in half and carve out the cores, making a nice scoop in the center. Brush with butter, then top with a sprinkle of sugar.
4. Put your cinnamon oat mixture into the centers of the pears.
5. Bake for 30-40 minutes, until soft.

Chocolate Peanut Butter Bites
Ingredients

- Chocolate chips of choice (2 c.)
- Coconut flour (1 c.)
- Honey (0.75 c.)
- Smooth peanut butter (2 c.)

Instructions

1. Prepare a tray with parchment paper to avoid sticking or messes
2. Melt together your peanut butter and honey, mixing well
3. Add coconut flour to peanut butter mixture and combine to incorporate. If it's still thin, add small amounts of flour. Let it thicken for 10 minutes.
4. Create 20 balls out of the dough.
5. Melt chocolate, then dip the dough balls into the chocolate and place them on the parchment. Refrigerate until firm.

Oatmeal Cookies
Ingredients

- Applesauce (2.5 Tbsp.)

- Baking soda (0.25 tsp)
- Coconut oil (2 Tbsp., melted)
- Dark chocolate chips (0.25 c.)
- Honey (0.25 c.)
- Salt (0.5 tsp)
- Vanilla extract (2 tsp.)
- Whole grain oats (0.5 c.)
- Whole wheat flour (0.5 c.)

Instructions

1. Set your oven to 350 F.
2. Mix syrup, oil (melted), applesauce, and vanilla.
3. Toss in salt, baking soda, oats, and flour. Combine well until it becomes a dough.
4. Mix the chocolate chips in.
5. Put in tablespoons onto cookie sheet.
6. Bake for 10 minutes. Let cool before transferring to a cooling rack.

Pina Colada Frozen Dessert
Ingredients

- Butter (0.25 c.)
- Crushed pineapple in juice (undrained—1 8 oz. can)
- Graham cracker crumbs (1.25 c.)
- Rum extract or rum (0.25 c.)
- Sugar (1 Tbsp.)
- Toasted flaked coconut (0.25 c.)
- Vanilla low-fat, no-sugar ice cream (4 c.)

Instructions

1. Prepare oven to 350 F.

2. Combine butter, cracker crumbs, and sugar. Press into a 2-quart baking dish. Bake 10 minutes and allow to cool completely
3. Combine ice cream, pineapple and juice, and extracts into a bowl with a mixer until well combined. Spread it out into the crust.
4. Freeze for 6 hours.
5. Serve after letting thaw for 5 minutes and topping with coconut shreds.

Kiwi Sorbet

Ingredients

- Kiwi (1 lb., peeled and frozen)
- Honey (0.25 c.)

Instructions

1. Combine everything well in a food processor until mixed.
2. Pour it into a loaf pan and smooth it out.
3. Allow it to freeze for 2 hours. Keep it covered if leaving it overnight in the freezer.

Ricotta Brûlée

Ingredients

- Ricotta cheese (2 c.)
- Lemon zest (1 tsp)
- Honey (2 Tbsp.)
- Sugar (2 Tbsp.)

Instructions

1. Mix together your ricotta, lemon zest, and honey. Then, split into ramekins. Top with sugar and place onto baking sheet.
2. Place oven rack at the topmost position then set the baking sheet in with the broiler on its highest setting. Watch closely and broil until it bubbles and turns golden brown—between 5 and 10 minutes.
3. Cool for 10 minutes and top with any fruits or toppings you prefer.

Chapter 4: Heart-Healthy Gourmet Meals

Grilled Halibut With Pine Nut Relish
Ingredients

- Diced red tomato (0.5 c.)
- Diced yellow tomato (o.5 c)
- EVOO (3 Tbsp.)
- Flour to coat fish
- Green olives (0.5 c.)
- Halibut fillet (4, 1 inch thick)
- Kalamata olives (0.5 c.)
- Lemon juice (1 Tbsp.)
- Zest from a lemon (0.5 tsp.)
- Parsley (2 Tbsp.)
- Pepper to taste
- Pine nuts (3 Tbsp.)
- Salt (pinch to taste)
- Shallot (1)

Instructions

1. Start with toasting the pine nuts in a dry skillet for a few minutes until toasted. Set aside.
2. Combine your tomatoes, the sliced olives, shallot, the lemon juice and zest, and 1 Tbsp. of oil. Mix well and add in parsley and a sprinkle of pepper.
3. Flour fillets, shaking off excess. Season lightly with salt and pepper. Toss the rest of your oil into your skillet and use that to cook the fish until done, flipping halfway over.
4. Serve with relish on top and garnish with pine nuts.

Shrimp Bowls
Ingredients

- Avocado (1, cut small)
- Broccoli (1 lb., florets)
- Ginger (1 Tbsp.)
- Olive oil (2 Tbsp.)
- Plum tomatoes (8 oz., seeds removed and cut)
- Quinoa (1.5 c.)
- Rice vinegar (1 Tbsp.)
- Salt and pepper to taste
- Scallions (2, thinly sliced)
- Shrimp (20 large, peeled and deveined)

Instructions

1. Warm oven to 425 F. Prepare medium saucepan at medium heat and cook the quinoa until toasted, roughly 5 minutes. Add in water (3 c.), then cover immediately. Allow it to cook just below a boil for 10 minutes, then take it off the burner and let it sit for another ten minutes.
2. On a baking sheet, add broccoli, 1 Tbsp. oil, salt, and pepper. Prepare in a single layer. Roast for 15 minutes. Season shrimp, then cook for 6-8 minutes, tossed with broccoli.
3. Mix vinegar, ginger, and remaining oil into a small bowl. Toss with tomatoes and scallions.
4. Serve with quinoa in bowls, topped with broccoli shrimp, then avocado. Finally, add the vinaigrette to the top.

Grilled Watermelon Steak Salad

Ingredients

- Cherry tomatoes (1 lb., halved)
- Honey (1 tsp)
- Lemon juice (3 Tbsp.)
- Mint leaves (1 c., torn up)
- Olive oil (2 Tbsp.)
- Onion (0.5 tsp., small red)
- Parsley (1 c., chopped)
- Salt and pepper
- Sirloin steak (1 lb.)
- Unsalted peanuts to garnish
- Watermelon (3 lbs., seedless)

Instructions

1. Prepare grill to medium-high. Season steak, then grill until done to preference. Allow it to rest on a cutting board.
2. Mix oil, lemon juice, honey, and seasonings. Incorporate the onions and tomatoes as well, folding in nicely.
3. Cut watermelon into 0.5-inch thick triangles and remove rinds. Oil and grill until starting to char—a minute per side, then set aside.
4. Mix the herbs into the tomato mixture. Serve with watermelon topped with stead.

Crispy Cod and Green Beans

Ingredients

- Green Beans (1 lb.)
- Olive oil (2 Tbsp.)
- Parmesan cheese (0.25 c., grated)
- Pepper to taste
- Pesto (2 Tbsp.)
- Salt to taste
- Skinless cod (1.25 lb., four pieces)

Instructions

1. Set oven to 425 F. Put beans onto rimmed baking sheet and combine with 1 Tbsp. oil, then top with cheese and a sprinkling of seasonings. Roast for 10-12 minutes, waiting for it to finally start to brown.
2. Heat remaining oil in a skillet. Season cod and cook until golden brown. You want to use a medium-high heat to do this.
3. Serve with pesto over cod, next to a bed of green beans.

Pistachio-Crusted Fish
Ingredients

- Baby spinach (4 c.)

- Greek yogurt (4 Tbsp.)
- Lemon juice (2 Tbsp.)
- Olive oil (2 Tbsp.)
- Panko (whole-wheat, 0.25 c.)
- Pepper (0.5 tsp)
- Quinoa (0.75 c.)
- Salt (0.75 tsp)
- Shelled pistachios, chopped (0.25 c.)
- Tilapia (4 6-oz. pieces)

Instructions

1. Prepare quinoa based on instructions on packaging.
2. Season fish with salt, pepper, and coat with 1 Tbsp. each of Greek yogurt.
3. Combine panko and pistachios, tossing with 1 Tbsp. olive oil. Gently sprinkle over the top of the fish, pressing it to stick. Bake for 12 minutes at 375 F., or until done.
4. Combine cooked quinoa with spinach, lemon juice, remaining oil, and a pinch of salt and pepper. Serve with fish.

Cumin-Spiced Lamb and Salad

Ingredients

- Carrots (1 lb.)
- Cumin (1.25 tsp.)
- Honey (0.5 tsp.)
- Lamb loin chops (8—about 2 lbs.)
- Mint leaves (0.25 c., fresh)
- Olive oil (3 Tbsp.)
- Radishes (6)
- Red wine vinegar (2 Tbsp.)
- Salt and pepper to taste

Instructions

1. Combine 2 Tbsp. oil, vinegar, a pinch of cumin, honey, and salt and pepper.
2. Warm remaining oil in a skillet at medium. Season lamb with cumin and a pinch of salt and pepper. Cook until preferred doneness.
3. Shave carrots into pieces and create thinly sliced radishes. Coat with dressing and mix with mint. Serve with lamb.

Chapter 5: Heart-Healthy Quick 'n Easy Meals

Sugar Snap Pea and Radish Salad

Ingredients

- Apple-cider vinegar (2 Tbsp.)
- Avocado (0.5, medium ripe)
- Dijon mustard (0.5 tsp)
- Fresh lemon juice (1 Tbsp.)
- Freshly ground pepper (0.5 tsp)
- Ground coriander (0.25 tsp)
- Olive oil (0.25 c.)

- Radishes (12, small)
- Salt (o.5 tsp)
- Sugar snap peas (1 lb.)
- Watermelon radish (1, small)

Instructions

1. Combine peas and radishes in a bowl together.
2. In a blender, combine everything else and puree until well combined and smooth. Add water if necessary to thin it out.
3. Coat radish and peas with dressing and serve.

Horseradish Salmon Cakes

Ingredients

- Dijon mustard (1 Tbsp.)
- English cucumber (1, small)
- Greek Yogurt (2 Tbsp.)
- Horseradish (2 Tbsp.)
- Lemon juice (1 Tbsp.)
- Olive oil (2 Tbsp.)
- Panko (0.25 c.)
- Salt and pepper to taste
- Skinless salmon filet (1.25 lb.)
- Watercress (1 bunch)

Instructions

1. Combine salmon, horseradish, salt and pepper, and mustard into a food processor until well chopped. Then, toss in the bread crumbs and combine well.
2. Form 8 patties.
3. Warm 1 Tbsp. oil in a skillet. Cook until opaque throughout, typically 2 minutes before flipping.
4. Combine yogurt, lemon juice, oil, and a sprinkle of salt and pepper. Combine in cucumber slices, then watercress.
5. Serve salmon with salad.

Salmon, Green Beans, and Tomatoes

Ingredients

- Garlic (6 cloves)
- Green beans (1 lb.)
- Grape tomatoes (1 pint)
- Kalamata olives (0.5 c.)
- Anchovy fillets (3)
- Olive oil (2 Tbsp.)
- Kosher salt and pepper to personal preference
- Salmon fillet, skinless

Instructions

1. Prepare oven to 425 F. Put beans, garlic, olive, anchovy, and tomatoes together along with half of the oil and a pinch of pepper. Roast until veggies are tender.
2. Warm the remainder of the oil over a skillet at medium heat. Season salmon, then cook until done. Serve salmon and veggies together.

Broccoli Pesto Fusilli
Ingredients

- Basil leaves (0.5 c.)

- Broccoli florets (12 oz.)
- Fusilli (12 oz.)
- Garlic (2 cloves)
- Lemon zest (1 Tbsp.)
- Olive oil (3 Tbsp.)
- Parmesan cheese to garnish
- Salt to taste
- Sliced almonds to garnish

Instructions

1. Prepare pasta to directions and reserve 0.5 c. of the liquid.
2. Combine broccoli, garlic, and the reserved water in a bowl and cook for five or six minutes, stirring halfway through. Put everything right into a food processor with the liquid. Combine in basil, oil, zest, a pinch of salt, and puree.
3. Put pasta in with pesto. Drizzle in water if necessary. Sprinkle with cheese and nuts if desired. Serve immediately.

Strawberry Spinach Salad

Ingredients

- Baby spinach (3 c.)
- Medium avocado (0.25, diced)
- Red onion (1 Tbsp.)
- Sliced strawberries (0.5 c.)
- Vinaigrette of choice (2 Tbsp.)
- Walnut pieces (roasted)

Instructions

1. Combine spinach with the berries and onion. Mix well. Coat with vinaigrette and toss. Then, top with walnuts and avocado. Serve.

One-Pot Shrimp and Spinach

Ingredients

- Crushed red pepper (0.25 tsp)
- Garlic (6 cloves, sliced)
- Lemon juice (1 Tbsp.)
- Lemon zest (1.5 tsp.)
- Olive oil (3 Tbsp.)
- Parsley (1 Tbsp.)
- Salt to personal preference
- Shrimp (1 lb.)
- Spinach (1 lb.)

Instructions

1. Warm skillet with 1 Tbsp. oil. Cook half of the garlic until browning, about a single minute. Then, toss in spinach and salt. Wait for it to wilt over the heat, about 5 minutes. Remove and mix in lemon juice, storing it in a separate bowl.
2. Warm heat to medium-high and toss with remainder of oil. Toss in the rest of your garlic and cook until browning. Then, mix in shrimp, pepper, and salt. Cook until shrimp is done, then serve atop spinach with lemon zest and parsley garnish.

Chapter 6: Heart-Healthy Vegetarian and Vegan Meals

Vegetarian Butternut Squash Torte

Ingredients

- Butternut squash (1 lb.)
- Crusty bread of choice
- Kale (1, small)
- Olive oil (1 Tbsp.)
- Parmesan cheese (4 Tbsp., grated)
- Plum tomato (1)
- Provolone cheese (6 oz., thinly sliced)
- Red onion (1, medium)
- Salt and pepper to taste
- Yukon Gold potato (1, medium)

Instructions

1. Take a spring form 9-inch pan and prepare it so that nothing will stick. Then, take your squash and put it around the bottom in circles to sort of mimic a crust.
2. Then, layer it with the onion, with the rings separated out.
3. Add half of your kale, then sprinkle half of your oil, and season to taste.
4. Then, layer with potatoes, half of your cheese, and top with the last of your kale.
5. Add the oil, onion, tomato slices, and the last of your cheese.
6. Top it with the remainder of your squash, then coat with parmesan.
7. Bake, covering the top with foil, for 20 minutes. Then, discard the foil and let it bake until it is tender and browning, typically another ten minutes or so.

Vegetarian Fried Rice

Ingredients

- 2 eggs (leave out if vegan)
- Garlic (2 cloves, pressed)
- Kale (6 oz., thinly sliced leaves)
- Olive oil (1 Tbsp.)
- Rice (4 c., cooked and chilled, preferably the day before)
- Sesame oil (1 Tbsp.)
- Shiitake mushroom caps (4 oz., sliced)
- Soy sauce (2 Tbsp., low sodium)
- Sriracha (1 tsp.)

Instructions

1. Start by warming your oil up in your pan of choice or wok. Your oil should be just before the smoking point.
2. Cook the mushrooms and toss until they start to turn golden brown, usually just a few minutes, then set them off for later.
3. Toss in some sesame oil and kale, cooking until wilted, then add in your garlic as well for another minute.
4. Take your rice and mix it in as well, tossing it together until heated.
5. Move all rice to the side, then pour beaten eggs in the center of your pan. Stir often until the eggs are just about finished, and then mix into the rice.
6. Mix in the soy sauce and sriracha, then top with mushrooms.

Vegan Butternut Squash Soup

Ingredients

- Butternut squash (1, 2.5 lbs. with skin and seeds removed—keep seeds)
- Carrots (2 medium, cut into 1-inch pieces)
- Coconut milk (2 Tbsp.)
- Olive oil (2 Tbsp., and one tsp)
- Onion (1, large, chopped)
- Pepper (2.25 tsp)
- Turmeric (2.25 tsp)
- Veggie bouillon base (1 Tbsp.)

Instructions

1. Take a Dutch oven and add 2 Tbsp. oil. Warm, then cook your onions until soft and translucent, roughly 6 minutes or so.
2. Integrate your bouillon base with 6 c., boiling water until completely dissolved.

3. Toss together your veggies, turmeric, and pepper into your onions in the Dutch oven. Allow it to cook for a minute before mixing in your veggie broth. Simmer for 20 minutes until veggies are soft.
4. Turn your oven to 375F. Take your seeds and your oil that is remaining and combine them together. Then, coat it up with the turmeric and pepper before toasting in your oven for about 1o minutes.
5. With a blender or immersion blender, combine your soup until smooth.
6. Serve topped with seeds and a swirl of coconut milk.

Vegetarian Kale and Sweet Potato Frittata

Ingredients

- Eggs (6)
- Garlic (2 cloves)
- Goat cheese (3 oz.)
- Half-and-half (1 c.)
- Kale (2 c., packed tightly)

- Olive oil (2 Tbsp.)
- Pepper (0.5 tsp.)
- Red onion (0.5, small)
- Salt (1 tsp.)
- Sweet potatoes (2 c.)

Instructions

1. With your oven warming, combine your eggs in a bowl. Then, add in the salt and half-and-half as well. Make sure your oven is at 350F.
2. In a nonstick skillet that you can put into your oven, cook your potatoes over 1 Tbsp. of oil. Wait for them to soften and start to turn golden. Then, remove from the pan.
3. Next, cook your kale, onion, and garlic together in the remainder of your oil until it is wilted and aromatic.
4. Put your potato back in with the kale, then pour your egg mix atop it all. Incorporate well and then allow it to cook on the stove for another 3 minutes.
5. Top it all with the goat cheese, then bake for 10 minutes until completely done.

Vegan Ginger Ramen
Ingredients

- Garlic (4 cloves, minced)
- Ginger (0.33 c., chopped coarsely)
- Grapeseed oil (0.5 c.)
- Low-sodium soy sauce (2 Tbsp.)
- Pepper (1 tsp., freshly ground)
- Ramen noodles (*real,* fresh noodles—not the $0.10 packaged stuff)
- Rice vinegar (1 Tbsp.)
- Salt to personal preference
- Scallions (1 bunch—about 2 c. sliced)
- Sesame oil (1 tsp)
- Sugar (0.5 tsp)

Instructions

1. Combine your ginger with the minced garlic and roughly 60% of your scallions.
2. Warm up the grapeseed oil until just before the smoking point. Then, take the oil and dump it over your scallion mix. It will sizzle and wilt, turning green. Leave it for 5 minutes, then add in the rest of the scallions.
3. Carefully combine in soy sauce, sesame oil, vinegar, sugar, and pepper, and leave it to incorporate for the next 15 minutes or so. Adjust flavor accordingly.
4. Prepare your noodles to the package instructions. Drain.
5. Introduce your noodles to your scallion sauce and coat well.
6. Serve topped with sesame seeds or any other toppings you may want.

Vegan Glazed Tofu
Ingredients

- Canola oil (0.5 c.)
- Firm tofu (12 oz.)
- Ginger (0.5" sliced thinly)
- Maple syrup (3 Tbsp.—you can use honey if you're not vegan.)
- Pepper flakes (0.5 tsp.)
- Rice vinegar (3 Tbsp.)
- Soy sauce (4 Tbsp.)
- Toppings of choice—recommended ones include rice, scallions, or sesame seeds

Instructions

1. Dry and drain your tofu out, squeezing it between paper towels so that you can remove as much of the liquid as you possibly can, then slice it into cubes.
2. Combine the wet ingredients together, and add in your pepper and ginger.
3. Warm your wok or skillet. When the oil is shimmery, gingerly place your tofu into it carefully and leave it for around 4 minutes so that it can brown. It should be dark brown when you flip. Repeat on both sides. Then, drop the heat down and toss in your sauce mix. Allow it to reduce until it is thick, roughly 4 minutes.
4. Put tofu on plates and top with anything you desire.

Vegan Greek Tofu Breakfast Scramble

Ingredients

- Basil (0.25 c., chopped)
- Firm tofu block (8 oz.)
- Garlic (2 cloves, diced)
- Grape tomatoes (0.5 c., halved)
- Kalamata olives (0.25 c., halved)
- Lemon juice (from ½ lemon)
- Nutritional yeast (2 Tbsp.)
- Olive oil (1 Tbsp.)
- Red bell pepper (0.5 c., chopped)
- Red onion (0.25, diced)
- Salt (pinch)
- Spinach (1 handful)
- Tahini paste (1 tsp)
- Salt and pepper to personal preference

Instructions

1. Break down tofu until the shape/texture of scrambled eggs. Then, combine in yeast, lemon juice, and tahini. Sprinkle with a pinch of salt.
2. Prepare skillet at a moderate heat. Sauté onions for 5 minutes before tossing in the pepper and garlic for an additional 5 minutes.
3. Mix in tofu and Kalamata olives. Warm through.
4. Toss in greens until wilted and reduced. Take off from heat and toss in tomatoes and season with salt and pepper to taste.

CPSIA information can be obtained
at www.ICGtesting.com
Printed in the USA
LVHW082139110321
681322LV00017B/548

9 789814 950787